THE BEST OF
Birds&Blooms

Downy woodpecker, page 66

Table of Contents

ON THE FRONT COVER
*Indigo bunting. Photo by Steve
and Dave Maslowski*

ON THE TITLE PAGE
*Northern cardinal. Photo by
John Clay*

A Birds & Blooms Book

© 2023 RDA Enthusiast
Brands, LLC.
1610 N. 2nd St., Suite 102,
Milwaukee, WI 53212-3906

**International Standard Book
Number:**
D 978-1-62145-898-2
U 978-1-62145-899-9

Component Number:
D 118500114H
U 118500116H

We are committed to both the
quality of our products and
the service we provide to our
customers. We value your
comments, so please feel free
to contact us at TMBBookTeam
@TrustedMediaBrands.com.

For more *Birds & Blooms* products
and information, visit our website:

www.birdsandblooms.com

Printed in USA
10 9 8 7 6 5 4 3 2 1

Text, photography and illustrations
for *The Best of Birds & Blooms*
are based on articles previously
published in *Birds & Blooms*
magazine (www.birdsandblooms
.com).

Contributors: Monica Cardoza,
Amy Grisak, Wendy Helfenbaum,
Heather Isherwood, Niki Jabbour,
Molly Jasinski, Ken and Kimberly
Kaufman, Ken Keffer, Rachael
Liska, Luke Miller, Eva Monheim,
Melinda Myers, Kelsey Roth, Sally
Roth, Jill Staake, Kaitlin Stanbrook,
Deb Wiley

Blue copper butterfly, page 134

Ruby-throated hummingbird, page 104

Welcome!

Immerse yourself in the world of birds, butterflies and much more with this latest edition of *The Best of Birds & Blooms*.

As always, the book features gorgeous photographs and fun facts along with practical birding and gardening advice. Did you know that some hummingbirds migrate almost 4,000 miles each year? Find out more about their amazing journeys on p. 112. What pollinator-friendly plants do best in low-light areas? Turn to p. 144.

Then head outside to observe the wonders in your own backyard.

—THE EDITORS OF
BIRDS & BLOOMS MAGAZINE

CHAPTER 1

Create a Backyard Bird Haven

*Attract more of your favorite species
with the right food and features*

Blooms for Birds

Zinnias are attractive to various seed-eating songbirds, but ruby-throated hummingbirds also stop by for nectar.

Attract goldfinches, cardinals and other eager seed eaters from summer through winter with a selection of annuals

Red Army
amaranth

Cosmos

Mourning doves temporarily store seeds in their crop—a pocket in their throat.

Indigo bunting on sunflower

FOR A BIG splash of color that lasts for months, you can't beat annual flowers.

Beauty is only the beginning. Once the blooms of graceful cosmos, cheerful sunflowers, dramatic dark-leaved amaranths, bold zinnias and other easy-to-grow annuals start to fade, the real fun begins. That's when they bring in the birds!

Even the best feeder foods often take a backseat to flower seeds. And watching a flock of goldfinches forage naturally among your plants is even more entertaining than seeing them on a tube feeder. That's true for the dozens of bird species that avidly eat the seeds of annuals, whether it's northern cardinals snapping up gomphrena, towhees carefully taking tithonia, or native sparrows and juncos energetically scratching beneath the marigolds.

Backyard Entertainment

Wildlife biologist Terry W. Johnson of Georgia marvels at the appeal. "When you see how small some of these seeds are, and how hard the cardinals work to get the tiny seeds when right nearby are black oil sunflower seeds at the feeder, it's amazing!" he says.

Annuals typically begin to attract songbirds in late summer, when the first flowers start to produce seeds. "If zinnias are blooming on your deck or in your garden, keep your eyes peeled for petals scattered beneath the plants," Terry urges. It's a clue that goldfinches have been enjoying a late-summer banquet, even before the seeds fully ripen. Terry sees the same telltale sign of bird activity beneath his containers of scarlet sage, a native wildflower that he has discovered is a favorite of northern cardinals.

Watch Closely

Seed eaters are surprisingly tricky to spot among flowers and foliage. Watch for motion—of both birds and plants. Willowy cosmos stems sway under the weight of goldfinches; marigolds and ornamental millet will bend to the ground as juncos and sparrows jump up to pull down seed heads; the flashes of wings will give away

ANNUAL FLOWERS FOR BIRDS

- Amaranth, any kind
- Brightest Brilliant Rainbow quinoa
- Calendula
- Celosia
- Cosmos
- Gomphrena (globe amaranth)
- Marigold
- Ornamental millet, such as Red Jewel or Purple Majesty
- Scarlet salvia (Salvia coccinea)
- Sunflower
- Tall verbena
- Tithonia
- Zinnia

Rose-breasted grosbeaks, such as this one in a crabapple, have strong beaks for eating seeds.

American goldfinch on zinnia

cardinals, jays, chickadees and others sampling the sunflowers.

"While I was gazing out the window over the kitchen sink, I saw the globe amaranth plants in one of our deck containers violently shaking," Terry says. "A female cardinal had landed on them and was pulling apart their flower heads! After tearing apart several blossoms to reach the tiny seeds hidden inside, the bird snipped off an entire flower head and flew away."

Because annuals put out new blossoms, and lots of them, the bird banquet lasts for months, long after the plants are hit by a killing frost. For gardeners who may be tempted to pull out the dead plants, "Simply resist the impulse to create a tidy garden," Terry says. "Let the plants remain standing if you want to add a new facet to bird feeding. You will be providing a great source of food, and you'll enjoy watching fascinating behavior."

Annuals for Every Space

Even a small bed of flowers will bring in the birds. So will container gardens, which Terry and his wife especially enjoy. "As we get older, our eyesight is not as good as it used to be," he says. "Containers bring wildlife closer to the window. We don't even have to go outside."

A bigger annual garden will attract more birds, and in more variety. Not only does it offer a lot of

seeds, but it also provides the sheltering cover that makes birds feel at home. Plant annuals around your birdbath, feeder area, garden gnome or other outdoor ornaments, and add containers of them to your garden beds. Human-made objects create a sense of orderliness, even in winter. The flower show may be finished, but songbirds will add a whole second act!

Try a variety of bird-favored annuals, but grow some of them in dense patches or rows of the same kind, instead of dotting them around. A concentrated swath of color looks great in bloom—and when seeds ripen, the patch provides the cover that songbirds seek. Be sure to plant some of your annuals a few feet from a favorite window or near an outdoor sitting area so you can watch birds seek out the seeds as long as they last.

EASY BIRD BUFFETS

Scatter annual seeds in a sunny spot and lightly cover them for blooms in as little as six weeks, or buy started plants. The most likely diners are goldfinches, native sparrows, juncos, towhees, northern cardinals and doves. Surprises such as grosbeaks, crossbills, buntings, redpolls or pine siskins may show up, too.

Intenz
Classic
celosia

Tufted titmouse

Create a Safe Bird Haven

Dish out seeds in a healthy environment

Black-capped chickadee on spruce tree

FEEDING BACKYARD birds is one of the greatest joys in life, but it's important to take steps to keep the birds healthy in the process. Use these tips to make your backyard an appealing and safe space.

Keep Things Clean

Dirty feeders can spread disease. Completely empty yours about once every two weeks, and more often in wet weather or if the food looks moldy. Take each feeder apart, then clean it thoroughly with dish soap and boiling water or a dilute bleach solution (one part bleach to nine parts water). Rinse the feeder well, dry it completely and refill with fresh seeds or other bird food. Clean hummingbird feeders and change the sugar water every three to five days.

Provide Window Warnings

Windows pose a huge risk by reflecting the sky or trees nearby, which invites birds to fly right into them. Researchers estimate that window collisions kill up to 1 billion birds a year, especially during migration season. New data indicates there is no truly safe distance from a window to put bird feeders. Instead, be sure to make any windows facing your feeders easy for birds to see. Deck these windows with specially designed anti-collision stickers, decals, bird tape or films that create an opaque surface outside. Or mark the window using bar soap in a grid pattern of 4 inches by 2 inches.

Protect from Predators

Feeders provide a quick lunch, but they also can turn diners into an easy meal for others. Add plenty of shelter nearby where backyard birds can escape when hawks circle above. Shrubs and trees are perfect choices. Foil ground predators such as foxes by hanging feeders high and using a squirrel baffle beneath. A cage-style feeder gives smaller birds an extra layer of protection while they feast. Always remember to keep pet cats indoors, too.

Grow Beneficial Plants

Birds rely on berries, seeds, nectar and the insects that plants attract. Grow native flowers, shrubs and trees in your yard to attract a wider variety of birds in every season. Visit your local nursery to ask for recommendations. Of course, avoid pesticides whenever possible.

Monitor Their Health

If you see birds that look ill—watch for crusty eyes, growths on their bodies or unusual behavior—take your feeders down immediately. Clean them thoroughly and wait several weeks before you put them back up. Keep an eye out for news stories about bird epidemics in your area and follow all recommendations to protect your feathery friends.

COVER CONIFERS

Plant these evergreens that offer protection.

Arborvitae

Colorado blue spruce

Common juniper

Mugo pine

Ponderosa pine

White pine

P.S. Dwarf varieties are great for small spaces, too!

HELP INJURED BIRDS

If you see a stunned bird that doesn't fly away when you approach, give it a quiet place to recover (such as a covered box) and immediately call a local wildlife rehabilitator.

Birdie Bath Time

These feathered friends usually skip stocked feeders,
but you can still attract them with fresh water

A brown thrasher, a bird not commonly seen at feeders, takes a dip in a birdbath.

Eastern
bluebird

BIRDBATH ESSENTIALS

Four top tips from Wild Birds Unlimited store owners Laura and Mel Tracy.

1. Change the water every few days and use a stiff brush to scrub off any debris.

2. Disinfect occasionally with a mild bleach solution (1 part bleach to 10 parts water) and rinse well.

3. Add the sound of moving water with a wiggler or dripper to attract migrating birds.

4. Heat birdbaths in the winter so visitors can clean and maintain their insulating feathers.

Summer tanager

WATER FEATURES—such as birdbaths, garden ponds and water fountains—are centerpieces of bird activity in yards, acting as safe places to get clean and sip fresh water. Add one to your space to attract these birds that usually turn up their beaks at any seed offerings, but can't resist taking a dip in a bird pool.

Tanagers

Western, scarlet and summer tanagers are some of the most tropical-looking species that appear in the United States and Canada, but they tend to stay up in the treetops. Providing water can lure them down and expand the variety of birds you see in your yard, according to Laura and Mel Tracy, owners of a Wild Birds Unlimited store in Palos Park, Illinois. They have had summer tanagers—and several species of warblers—come to their birdbath.

Thrushes

American robins are the most familiar of these hefty, long-legged songbirds. Varied thrushes are common in the dense wet woods of the Pacific Northwest. Veery and wood thrushes boast rich cinnamon hues, while hermit and Swainson's thrushes are more olive in tone. Depending on the area, several kinds of thrushes can show up in yards during migration. As insect and berry specialists, thrushes aren't particularly drawn to feeders, but they will slurp water from a birdbath.

Bluebirds

While bluebirds are also members of the thrush family, they're special enough to merit their own category. They may take mealworms from a feeder, but a birdbath is far more attractive to western, eastern and mountain bluebirds—especially during cold snaps. The Tracys point out that Bluebirds, robins and many other birds aren't able to eat snow as cold-weather species such as juncos can. Set up a heated birdbath to keep water available year-round, even on days with freezing temperatures, to help these birds stay hydrated.

Wood thrush

Golden-crowned kinglet

Cedar waxwings

Kinglets

Tiny, active ruby-crowned and golden-crowned kinglets get their abundance of energy from scarfing insects high in the trees. Moving water may bring them down from the canopy, but they won't sit still long. After a brief refresh session at the water, kinglets will vanish just as quickly as they appeared.

Vireos

The birds in this musical group are noted for their near-constant singing from the treetops. A thicker bill helps distinguish vireos from other insect eaters. A simple water dish might not be enough to attract vireos, so consider a flowing fountain instead. Moving water cuts down on mosquito egg-laying and may even attract hummingbirds.

Thrashers

Providing shelter is another key element for successfully attracting water lovers, especially for thicket-dwelling fliers such as thrashers. Entice them by situating a birdbath near cover. Easy access to trees and shrubs protects all songbirds from predators. Wet birds cannot fly well, so they need a place to preen themselves and stay safe, according to the Tracys.

Waxwings

Both cedar and Bohemian waxwings are noted berry lovers. They travel in flocks, so sheltered perching locations and fruit-producing trees and shrubs attract these elegant visitors. After they gorge themselves on juniper, mountain ash, hawthorn or holly berries, entice them closer to the ground with a water feature.

Wrens

House, Pacific and winter wrens hop and crawl through thickets as they forage. Look for the perky behavior and striped eyebrow of Carolina wrens in the east and Bewick's wrens in the west. The Tracys say that it's best to place birdbaths where you can see them to maximize your enjoyment of watching the birds, and also as a reminder to maintain your birdbath regularly.

PICK THE BEST BASIN

The most ideal birdbaths are about 20 inches in diameter with a depth of around 2 inches. Concrete and fiberglass blends and thick plastic baths tend not to crack in winter.

Red-eyed
vireo

Meals on the Fly

Attract insect-loving birds that search midair, in leaf litter and tall grass, on foliage and branches, or beneath tree bark for their next meal

BLUEBIRDS

Nesting boxes will attract bluebirds to your yard, but the bugs keep them there. With short, slender bills that are ideal for snatching insects, these dazzling thrushes pluck beetles from veggie gardens, catch mosquitoes and moths out of the air, and study the ground from a low perch for grasshoppers, crickets and beetles in tall grass. Eastern and western bluebirds spot caterpillars and insects in grass more than 50 yards away. "Birds are primarily visual hunters," says Desiree L. Narango, a postdoctoral researcher at the University of Massachusetts, Amherst. "When insects come out, birds key in on them right away."

DO BIRDS EAT BEES?

Birds that eat bees only do it occasionally. "In general, bees are not highly preferred insects," Desiree says. Eastern kingbirds, scarlet tanagers and summer tanagers will eat bees whenever the opportunity arises, but most birds do not seek them out. The majority of birds that prey on bees catch the insects while in flight and consume them whole.

Eastern bluebird

Carolina
chickadee

Eastern phoebe

Phoebes

Unsurprisingly, these members of the flycatcher family "eat mostly aerial insects," Desiree says. The brownish gray eastern phoebe and the light brown western species, Say's phoebe, take short flights from a favorite perch, snatch a mosquito or fly midair, then, in a flash, return to their landing pad. "In the fall, when it's warm, they'll gobble down lots of yellow jackets and flies," she says.

Nuthatches

These gray-blue birds travel headfirst down tree trunks, probing the bark with their long, thin bills for beetles, treehoppers, ants, caterpillars and scale insects that woodpeckers may have missed. Pygmy and brown-headed nuthatches even craft tools from bark bits to pry up and expose insects. In summer, they're drawn to leafy backyards to forage for critters.

Chickadees

During spring and summer, insects make up the vast majority of black-capped chickadees' diet. "Even in winter, more than 50% of their diet is insects overwintering in dead leaves or in bark," Desiree says. These agile birds catch flies and moths in open air; glean aphids, scale insects and beetles from plants; and store the insects in crevices or under twigs.

Brown-headed nuthatch

DO BIRDS EAT MOSQUITOES?

Many common birds, such as northern cardinals and house sparrows, occasionally eat mosquitoes. But barn swallows, blackpoll warblers and eastern phoebes are mosquito-eating champions.

Rose-breasted grosbeak

DO BIRDS EAT BUTTERFLIES?

Orioles, grosbeaks, blue jays and other birds will occasionally go after butterflies and their caterpillars, whose bodies are nutritious. But adult butterflies' size make them difficult for small birds to catch. "For the most part, moths are more abundant and palatable than butterflies," says Desiree.

Grosbeaks

Thick, conical bills are ideal for cracking tough seeds as well as grasshoppers, crickets and other insects with tough exoskeletons. Rose-breasted grosbeaks and their western cousins, black-headed grosbeaks, fly out to capture bugs, such as wasps, bees and flies, and pick up beetles in foliage and branches. Their diet is half insects during the breeding season, with seeds and fruit rounding off the rest of the menu.

Northern Flickers

Northern flickers eat beetles and grasshoppers, but their favorite insects are ants—they can eat over a thousand in a single day. In addition to drilling into wood for bugs as other members of the woodpecker family do, flickers hammer at the soil for ants and their larvae. Desiree says, "Most woodpeckers key in on bark beetles and wood-boring beetles and eat ants on occasion, but they don't target them as the flicker does."

Northern flicker

Ruby-throated
hummingbird

Tufted Titmice

They're a familiar sight at seed feeders, but the gray-crested birds are also found upside-down or sideways on branches searching for caterpillars, ants, aphids and treehoppers, as well as wasps and stink bugs. When tufted titmice aren't hanging around, they're often hopping on the ground searching for insects, which make up most of their diet in summer.

Hummingbirds

With an amazing ability to hover and quickly change direction, hummingbirds catch gnats, mosquitoes, aphids, mites and flying ants while on the move—even from spider webs without becoming entangled themselves. They swallow their prey whole, since their long, narrow bill prevents them from manipulating or tearing apart their food. Put out overripe bananas to attract fruit flies and draw in hummingbirds.

Tufted
titmouse

White-breasted
nuthatch

Ready, Set, Crunch!

The big benefits of serving black oil sunflower seeds in your backyard

Purple finch

WE ALL HAVE OPINIONS on the best ways to attract feathered friends. But we can all agree on one thing: The greater variety of birds, the better. Serve up black oil sunflower seeds, also called oilers, and you have a pretty good chance at a big payoff.

Low Risk, High Reward

Birds focus on foods that have a big return on investment. So setting out seeds that are high in fat, such as black oil sunflower seeds, is an easy way to help birds enjoy a nutrient-dense snack, especially during the breeding season and winter weather.

According to the Cornell Lab of Ornithology, black oil sunflower seeds have thin shells, making them easier to crack open than striped sunflower seeds.

"Black oil sunflower seeds are related to regular sunflower seeds, but they've been cultivated to have a higher fat content," says John Rowden, the senior director of bird-friendly communities at the National Audubon Society.

If you prefer to buy the striped variety, ensure that the seeds are approved for wildlife and are unsalted and unseasoned.

Serve up Seeds

To offer the high-fat treats safely and reduce seed spoilage, try tube feeders, recommends David Bonter, the co-director of the Cornell Lab's Center for Engagement in Science and Nature. "They help keep the seed dry. We don't want birdseed to get wet, because mold can form that is harmful to birds," he says.

Often, birders put out shelled oilers to minimize the mess. Because both sunflower hearts and chips quickly spoil, only dish out an amount that backyard birds can consume in a couple of days.

Keep It Fresh

If you notice stale or moldy seeds, David recommends sanitizing the feeder with soap, water and a 10% bleach solution.

If you're not sure if it's time to replace the seeds, David says, "have the birds tell you—birds tend to avoid seeds that have gone bad."

Sow Your Own

Common sunflowers, such as the one shown here, are closely related to black oil sunflowers and are easy to find and grow. Plant them for a simple way to add another food source to your yard for visiting wild birds.

"Planting sunflowers in the backyard also provides host opportunities for insects, and the birds can then forage on them," John says.

SUNFLOWER SEED LOVERS

Cardinals
Chickadees
Finches
Grosbeaks
Jays
Mourning doves
Nuthatches
Titmice
Woodpeckers

Birding in a Winter Wonderland

Birders have no need to go into hibernation this season. Use these easy tricks to see even more fliers when the mercury drops.

Blue jay on American bittersweet

Blue jays, northern cardinals and a black-capped chickadee share a feeder.

FEEDER ACTIVITY ISN'T ALWAYS consistent throughout the year. You may notice an uptick in guests in the winter, because a lot of natural food is frozen or hidden under blankets of snow. Birds are generally less territorial in the nonbreeding season, too, so they are more tolerant of sharing space at the feeder.

So it's time to top off the seed supply, pour yourself a cup of hot cocoa, and enjoy the snow birds with these top tips and tricks for winter bird-watching.

Focus on Feeders

Many birds grow extra down feathers in winter. The puffed-up feathers provide insulation against the elements. Yet winter is still a battle for survival for birds. Feeders with high-fat foods such as suet and peanuts give feathered friends a boost. Woodpeckers are especially fond of these calorie-rich treats, so to attract them to your yard, consider a double suet feeder or one with a long tail prop that allows them to use their tails as a tripod as they feed. Planting native berry-producing shrubs also provides much-needed nutrients for many species as winter settles in.

Eastern bluebird

Carolina wren at suet feeder

Wet Their Whistle

Water is an especially attractive offering that entices birds during the colder months. Adding a heater keeps your birdbath from icing over, giving birds a dependable place to get a drink (although they won't use it like a birdie hot tub to warm up). Beyond the backyard, natural areas with open water are magnets for birds in winter. Congregations of waterfowl flock to large rivers and coastal areas. Use your car as a portable blind while you scope for large groups of cold-tolerant ducks, geese and swans.

Add Roosting Boxes

Bird boxes are often associated with the nesting season, but nuthatches, chickadees, wrens and others will utilize them as roosting sites in the winter. Roosting boxes provide sheltered spots that are warmer than the bone-chilling outside air. Natural shelters, such as cavities in dead or living trees and dense thickets of conifers, can give a similar refuge to smaller birds such as tiny northern saw-whet owls.

Wait for Blustery Days

A bird's diet is mostly from natural sources, such as berries, seeds and nuts, even when food is scarce. But blizzards and winter storms often bring visitors to feeding stations. Bundle up and top off your feeders repeatedly after bad weather. The birds' easy access to a birdseed buffet after a storm provides some of the best bird-watching opportunities. For example, flocks of grosbeaks might ignore feeders much of the season, but they tend to show up during the worst weather. Providing additional feeding stations can help accommodate these occasional large flocks.

Go for a Drive

Some of the best birding can happen from the comfort of your car. Roll your windows down and crank your heaters up. After the autumn leaves fall, the open canopy makes spotting wildlife a bit easier. Look for owls and hawks in the treetops as you cruise the back roads. Migrants that breed on the tundra, from longspurs to snowy owls, often find winter refuge along plowed fields and roadside ditches. Snow buntings will mix in with flocks of horned larks, too.

Welcome Snow Birds

Even in the northern reaches of the continent, winter brings new migrants. Dark-eyed juncos, for example, are exclusively winter backyard visitors for many folks. These sparrow relatives are predominantly ground feeders, but they also eat from platform trays and fly-through feeders. Look for streaked pine siskins among the goldfinches—they'll blend into goldfinches wearing their more drab winter feathers. The anticipation of irruptive migrants is another winter highlight—you never know if it will be the year a redpoll shows up in your neighborhood.

Bird for a Cause

Get involved with a community science project. Project FeederWatch runs from November to April. You can count the birds in your own yard or another designated location. The Audubon Christmas Bird Count is also wonderful for the camaraderie, in addition to being one of the longest-running citizen science programs. Or opt for the Great Backyard Bird Count, an annual four-day event held each February. Beyond data collection, many of these events hold online photo contests and offer other ways to get involved and interact with fellow winter bird-watchers.

House finch

Dark-eyed junco

JOIN THE FESTIVITIES

*From warm oases to frigid destinations, all corners of the United States offer
a winter birding festival.*

- **Birds on the Niagara**
  Buffalo area, New York

- **Everglades Birding Festival**
  Davie, Florida

- **San Diego Bird Festival**
  San Diego, California

- **Whooping Crane Festival**
  Port Aransas area, Texas

- **Winter Wings Festival**
  Klamath Falls, Oregon

Please check festival websites for details and any COVID-19 updates.

Slather peanut butter on a pine cone, then roll it in birdseed for a fun way to feed black-capped chickadees and other hungry feathered fliers.

Cold-Weather Cuisine

Choose high-energy foods to keep backyard birds well fed during winter

FORAGING IS tough business with snow on the ground, which is why our wintertime bird visitors benefit from high-energy food options.

Even during subzero conditions, birds have special ways of keeping warm. Some fliers, such as finches and chickadees, pack on as much as 10% body fat from eating berries and insects in fall to build up their winter stores.

But many visitors appreciate an extra food boost. Plan ahead to keep your backyard birds fed when the weather turns cool.

Top-Tier Seeds

"When the weather is colder, the birds appreciate those fatty seeds," says Emma Greig, project leader for Project FeederWatch at the Cornell Lab of Ornithology. She notes that fat is critical for meeting birds' caloric needs.

"An easy bird feed is black oil sunflower seeds," Emma says. The seed is popular with most birds that winter in the northern regions and is typically easy to find in feed stores or even grocery stores.

Safflower seeds are favorites for northern cardinals and grosbeaks. Emma also recommends thistle seeds (sometimes called Nyjer seeds), which attract finches, pine siskins, dark-eyed juncos, and other smaller foragers.

Savory Suet

Because animal fat is easily digestible, suet cakes provide important calories for a wide variety of birds. Offer it in a mesh bag or a suet feeder suspended out of reach of other curious wildlife.

Peanut-Palooza

Don't forget about peanuts. Jays and woodpeckers prefer whole peanuts, while nuthatches and chickadees like the shelled version. Emma says peanut butter is another excellent fat source for birds. Either mix it with suet or by spreading it on pine cones or along tree bark.

Fruit Fans

Some birds, such as robins and cedar waxwings, enjoy dried cranberries, currants and raisins. Offer them in a suet cake or on a platform feeder after soaking them in water for a few hours to soften.

For an even easier food source, Emma says, "Grow a few trees and shrubs that have berries in the winter." Chokecherry, hawthorn, snowberry and Rocky Mountain juniper are all good choices.

Even when the chilly months seem to roll on, it's simple and fun to provide backyard birds with a high-energy buffet while also enjoying a wintry bird fix right outside your windows.

Eastern bluebird

WELCOMING WATER
Give birds a place to drink during the cold months with a heated birdbath.

SUET ENTHUSIASTS
These birds can't get enough of this snack.

Blue jays
Cardinals
Chickadees
Nuthatches
Pine warblers
Ruby-crowned kinglets
Tufted titmice
Woodpeckers
Wrens

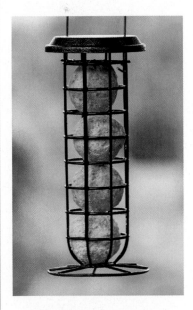

COME AND GET IT
Host a wide array of birds with a suet ball and feeder combo set.

CHAPTER 2

Birds
In-Depth

*Explore the fascinating characteristics
of some amazing species*

The Young and the Nestless

It's a big world out there—learn how baby birds hatch and grow before gaining their independence and taking flight

A male northern cardinal with a fledgling.

ONE OF THE MOST fascinating elements of bird-watching is the opportunity to watch your feathered neighbors raise their young. In North America, most birds nest in late spring and summer, but some activity—adult birds building nests, laying eggs and raising young—happens during every season. Baby birds can appear almost anywhere, including in small backyards or city parks. Here are answers to the most common questions about these adorable youngsters.

What's the correct term for baby birds?

It's fine just to call them babies, chicks or youngsters. To be more specific, a young bird that has just hatched out of the egg is a hatchling, one that's still in the nest is a nestling and a young bird that has left the nest is known as a fledgling.

When and how do birds hatch?

Some birds, such as great horned owls, can hatch as early as January in certain parts of the southern U.S. But American goldfinches may hatch as late as September.

Before eggs can hatch, they must be incubated. The warmth of incubation helps the embryo to develop inside the egg. Many small songbirds need only 11 to 14 days of incubating before hatching. Some large birds, such as hawks or geese, take about a month to hatch, and it's as much as 80 days for huge seabirds such as albatrosses.

When a female bird lays a clutch of eggs, she may delay incubation until the clutch is complete so that all the eggs will hatch at around the same time. However, barn owls begin incubating after laying the first egg and may lay up to seven eggs at intervals of two or three days. So their eggs hatch one at a time, with the first hatchlings much larger than their younger siblings.

Are there different kinds of baby birds?

Definitely! Scientists divide baby birds into two broad types. The first, altricial young, such as those of most songbirds and hummingbirds,

Great horned owlets huddle together in their nest tucked into a tree.

BABY BIRD TIMELINE

Follow the journey of young robins.

DAY 1
Female robin begins building her cup-shaped nest out of twigs and grass with a mud base.

DAY 8
Female lays first egg.

DAY 9
Lays second egg.

DAY 10
Lays third egg. Female may begin incubating.

Actual size

DAY 11
Lays fourth egg. Female commits to incubating.

Continued on p. 45.

hatch naked and with their eyes closed. Scrawny, pink and helpless, they can barely raise their heads at first. The other type, precocial young, such as those of ducks and chickens, are covered with down when they hatch. As soon as they dry off, often within a couple of hours, they are alert, active, and able to get up and walk around.

How long does it take young birds to leave the nest?

This varies a lot depending on the species. Young born with down feathers may leave the nest to follow their parents within a few hours after hatching, as is the case for baby ducks, plovers or pheasants. Small songbirds develop rapidly thanks to their hardworking parents constantly bringing them food. They may leave the nest eight to 12 days after hatching. Some big birds develop much more slowly. For example, the California condor, one of our largest North American birds, may not leave the nest until it's 6 months old.

How do young birds learn to fly?

Many songbirds can barely fly when they leave the nest. Young northern cardinals depart the nest at only 7 to 9 days old and may not be able to fly well for another week or more. But they usually get around well enough to avoid predators and find food.

On the other hand, baby barn swallows may not leave the nest until 20 days after they hatch. Swallows feed on flying insects that they grab in midair, and young barn swallows wait until their wings are fully developed before they take off. For swallows, swifts and hawks, flight is such an essential part of their lifestyle that the young stay close to their parents at first and may learn to fly partly from watching them.

What do baby birds eat and how do they learn to eat on their own?

Some species' chicks hatch out of the egg with the instinct to find their own food. Young sandpipers and ducklings will start pecking at tiny insects within hours of hatching. Baby quail run after their parents, who show them how to nibble on insects and seeds, and soon the hatchlings begin to find food for themselves.

But birds that hatch naked sit in the nest and wait for their parents to bring them food. For most songbird nestlings, the diet consists mainly of protein-rich insects, even if the adults tend to be seed-eaters for much of the year. Cedar

waxwings bring insects to their young for the first two days, but then start bringing a variety of fruits. American goldfinch babies get a diet of mashed-up seeds. After young birds leave the nest they may watch how their parents search for food, but mostly they will learn by trial and error, with instinct sharpened by practice.

How do young birds take care of themselves after they're away from their parents?

Life is tough for young birds when they're first apart from their parents. They have to figure out how to find enough food to keep up their strength, while learning how to recognize predators and other potential dangers. If they can survive their first few weeks of independence, however, they have a good chance of living a normal life span.

Support young birds where you live by providing native plants, keeping cats indoors and avoiding pesticides. In return, you'll get the excitement of watching young birds as they grow up and explore their world.

Mallard ducklings are ready to leave their nest within hours of hatching.

A female Anna's hummingbird cares for her young nestlings.

Continued from p. 43.

DAY 22
First egg begins to hatch.

DAY 24
Last egg finishes hatching. Female broods newly hatched young to keep them warm. Both parents bring food for the young.

DAY 37
All young begin to leave the nest. Adults continue to feed them as they explore the surrounding area.

DAY 58 TO DAY 65
Young robins become independent.

Juvenile robin

A True Blue Trio

Find out which of the three North American bluebirds call your area home, and learn how to win them over with the right food and habitat

A male eastern bluebird feeds a mealworm to his mate as they perch on a crabapple.

Eastern bluebird
with fledglings

ONE LOOK AT A BLUEBIRD with its vibrant colors, and it's easy to see why the birds rank near the top of any list of best-loved birds. Classified as thrushes, a family found worldwide, the three bluebird species are unique to North America.

All three are medium-small songbirds that live in open habitats. Male bluebirds are more brightly colored than females, and juveniles wear a pattern of spots, reflecting their thrush ancestry. Insects make up most of their summer diet, but the birds wander in flocks in winter, eating small fruits and berries.

The Classic: Eastern Bluebird

The most widespread member of this trio is the eastern bluebird. In summer, it lives throughout southeastern Canada and in the United States east of the Rocky Mountains. A separate population is found from southern Arizona through Mexico and into Central America.

Many eastern bluebirds migrate in fall, and the species becomes more common in central and southern states in winter. A few stay through the cold months as far north as Canada. These wintering bluebirds move around the countryside in small flocks, gathering to feed on the fruits of poison ivy, dogwood, holly, and other vines and trees.

Eastern bluebirds are easy to identify by their upright posture, color pattern and thin, straight bills. Adult males are deep blue on the head, back, wings and tail; rusty orange on the chest; and white on the lower belly. Adult females have the same pattern in muted colors.

Western bluebird

Mountain bluebird on locust tree

Earth Tones: Western Bluebird

This species replaces the eastern bluebird in areas west of the Great Plains. In the Southwest, it's mostly a bird of foothills and mountains. Along the Pacific Coast, it tends to live in parks and yards.

While it looks similar to the eastern bluebird, they have differences. The male usually has a patch of rusty brown across the middle of its blue back, and its throat is blue. The lower belly is gray, not white. Female western bluebirds are similar to males, but with the blue mostly replaced by gray.

In winter, western bluebirds may gather in large flocks, especially in foothills with a crop of juniper berries. They also move out into desert areas to feed on the fruits of mistletoe growing on mesquite trees.

Sky Blue Flier: Mountain Bluebird

Despite the name, mountain bluebirds are not just creatures of high elevations. Instead, they actually favor open country with few trees. In summer, they can be found in meadows above the timberline of western mountains, and on lowland prairies as far east as the Dakotas and as far north as Alaska. In winter, they move in flocks through the Southwest and the southern Great Plains. As the most strongly migratory bluebirds, they stray out of range and have been spotted in almost all the eastern states.

Mountain bluebirds appear lighter and airier than the two other species. Males are pale sky blue and females are pale gray, both without rusty tones. They're more buoyant in flight, too. They have longer wings and tails, and can hover in one spot, gracefully beating their wings, for up to a minute. While eastern and western bluebirds perch on a branch before dropping to the ground to pick up insects, mountain bluebirds can hover above the grass and watch for their tiny prey.

Attracting and Helping Bluebirds

Unlike other thrushes, bluebirds nest in tree holes—either natural cavities or old woodpecker holes. This creates problems for the bluebirds in areas where people have removed dead trees, which are ideal for such cavities. The birds also compete with aggressive house sparrows and European starlings for nesting sites.

But over the past few decades, dedicated fans have put out thousands of nesting boxes, either singly or in bluebird trails along country roads. These boxes have helped all three species thrive.

In addition to nesting sites, native plants that provide the fruits they love will attract more bluebirds. Junipers, dogwoods, sumacs, hollies, serviceberries and elderberries are good choices. Water is another magnet for bluebirds; a source of clean, unfrozen water is welcome in all seasons. And although bluebirds ignore most feeder fare, they eagerly gobble up mealworms.

Wherever you live, at least one of the bluebird species can be found nearby, and it's worth the effort to attract these beautiful visitors.

BUILD IT AND THEY WILL COME
Help local bluebirds with a nest box.

The ideal box has an entrance hole 1.5 inches in diameter and is designed to be easily opened for cleaning. Place the box on a post in an open area, about 5 feet above the ground, with a predator guard on the post to keep intruders from climbing up.

Eastern bluebird

Defying Gravity

Moving headfirst down tree trunks is just one nuthatch trait. Find out more about this fun-to-watch bird family.

White-breasted nuthatches are year-round residents and frequent feeders in much of the United States.

Notice the size difference between a white-breasted nuthatch (left) and a red-breasted nuthatch (right).

THE ONLY BIRDS that routinely forage upside down, short-legged and stubby-tailed nuthatches are built for hugging tree bark while peering into crevices for bugs.

A quick jab with their long bills, and insect eggs, larvae, cocoons or adult bugs become their next meal. The birds are doing the trees a favor—all that foraging protects the trees from pests.

Nuthatches might be oddballs in their upside-down foraging habits, but at the feeder, their favorite foods are familiar. The first clue is in their name: Nuts are number one! Chopped nuts (especially peanuts) and sunflower seeds are their mainstays. The birds welcome suet, peanut butter and mealworms, too. At feeders, nuthatches often grab and go, carrying the nuts and seeds away to hack up elsewhere. Unlike jays or chickadees, they don't hold their food with their feet to work at it. Instead, they wedge the nut or seed into a crevice so it will stay put while they hammer away, chipping it into bite-sized bits with their bills. They also cache food by hammering it into cracks.

All nuthatches have the same shape, with blue-gray backs and lighter bellies (females are paler than males). Quick and agile, nuthatches are some of the most entertaining backyard fliers.

White-Breasted Nuthatch

The biggest of the bunch, this 5½-inch species may be mistaken for a woodpecker—until its habit of going down tree trunks headfirst gives it away. Stark white below, it's a year-round sight across the country, appearing singly or in pairs on deciduous or coniferous trees and making loud, nasal *yank-yank* calls.

White-breasted nuthatches frequent feeders and may adopt a nest box, since they prefer to use an existing cavity rather than chisel out their own. In winter, pairs often join a foraging flock of chickadees and other small birds.

Red-Breasted Nuthatch

This little nuthatch, with a rusty breast and a white stripe above the eye, is remarkably unafraid of people. Seen year-round in western and northern forests, it's the only migratory nuthatch. Some don't migrate at all, others make short journeys, and during a thrilling irruption year, big numbers of red-breasteds move south as far as the Gulf Coast.

RED-BREASTED NUTHATCHES live year-round in Canada and parts of the western U.S. They may show up almost anywhere in the U.S. in migration.

PYGMY NUTHATCHES are mostly permanent residents of the western mountains in the U.S.

Everything this bird does is rapid, including its yammering *eng-eng-eng* call, except when they know a hawk is around. Then it freezes like a statue until the coast is clear. Seen singly or in pairs except during migration, these birds eagerly come to feeders.

Red-breasteds dig their own nest holes, and then smear conifer sap around the entrance, sometimes using a flake of bark as a tool to spread the sticky stuff. The sap deters predators but doesn't hinder the nuthatches, which dive straight in without first pausing to perch.

Pygmy Nuthatch

Look for groups of the smallest nuthatch, only 4 inches long, in western forests of ponderosa and other pines. Pygmy nuthatches have a pale cinnamon breast and grayish brown cap. And they are talkative! Keeping up a constant *pip-pip-pip-pippety*, the sociable birds roam about in search of insects and pine seeds and visit feeders for the usual nuthatch treats.

Pygmy nuthatches may dig out a new nest cavity or adapt an existing one. Their relatives, especially their young male offspring, serve as nest helpers to defend and feed the brood.

On brutally cold nights, the flock—which can number more than 100 in winter—roosts together in a tree cavity, with birds crowding in by the dozens and lowering their body temperature so they need fewer calories to keep them alive.

Brown-Headed Nuthatch

Squeeze a squeaky toy repeatedly as fast as you can, and you'll have an idea of this species' voice.

Look up to find small groups in the pine forests of the Southeast, usually high in the trees.

A little over 4 inches long with a rich brown cap, the brown-headed nuthatch often uses a flake of bark as a tool, lifting other pieces to reveal insects. Nuts and sunflower seeds are a hit at feeders, and a nest box may get takers. Again, watch for nest helpers, usually young males, that assist the others with feeding and defense.

BROWN-HEADED NUTHATCHES can be found year-round in pine forests of the southeastern U.S.

A Thrill of Color

Buntings always stand out in a crowd—learn where to find them and the field marks that set these birds apart

Painted bunting on elbow bush
(Forestiera pubescens)

Indigo bunting

Lazuli bunting

ONE THING'S FOR SURE: When it comes to beauty and variety, it's tough to beat the buntings. They are found in a wide array of North American locations, from the high arctic tundra to the low country of the Southeast. The coloration of these birds is as distinct as their ranges. Males show everything from stark black and white palettes to a rainbow of colors. Females tend to have more subtle hints of coloring. Some buntings are related to sparrows or longspurs, while others are kin to cardinals and grosbeaks, yet another sign of their diversity. Learn more about these bright birds and where to find them.

Blue Beauties

The most widespread group, indigos are the buntings of the East. Their core breeding range stretches from southern Quebec to central Florida and west all the way to Arizona and New Mexico. Look for bright blue males singing cheery paired notes from perches in brushy fields or woodland edges.

Predominately brown, tan and white, females and young males show hints of blue feathering. Like most other buntings, male indigos molt into a more subdued winter plumage. During migration, the blotchy birds can play tricks on even the most talented birder's eyes, as the feather coloring doesn't match up with anything in field guides. Indigo buntings will occasionally visit thistle-seed feeders, so be on the lookout, especially in spring.

Jewels of the West

Search for flashy lazuli buntings throughout the western United States. Jacelyn Downey, education programs manager for Audubon Rockies, sees lazuli buntings near her Wyoming home close to the Black Hills. "If you're just glancing, you could easily mistake the male lazuli bunting for an eastern or western bluebird," she says.

Lark bunting

The name lazuli refers to the stunning blue lapis lazuli gemstone. The male's blue is offset with a rusty brown chest band and a white belly. Wing bars—white in males, buffy cinnamon on the females—help distinguish the lazulis from indigo buntings. Crossbreeding between the two birds is fairly common in the Great Plains, where their ranges overlap.

Rainbow of Color

Jacelyn occasionally would see colorful painted buntings, with feathers in shades of blue, green, red and yellow, when she lived in Louisiana. "You can't fully appreciate them in the shade, but when the light hits the males just right, you wonder why all birds don't look like that," she says.

The main breeding range of painted buntings is the south-central United States. Additionally, an eastern population nests from coastal North Carolina to central Florida. Painteds may winter from southern Florida to Panama. The birds often forage in dense stands of vegetation but can sometimes be seen in the open at feeding stations, where they'll eat thistle or white millet seed.

"It seems as though, in so many cases, we've

trained our brains to think that the way a bird looks is the male version of the species," Jacelyn says. But females and young male painted

BUNTING HOT SPOTS
Head to one of these locations for prime birding opportunities.

INDIGO
Cuyahoga Valley National Park, Ohio

LAZULI
Glacier National Park, Montana

PAINTED
Holla Bend National Wildlife Refuge, Arkansas

LARK
Pawnee National Grassland, Colorado

SNOW
Arctic National Wildlife Refuge, Alaska

VARIED
Big Bend National Park, Texas

buntings are also appealing with feathers that have a greenish tint.

Formal Feathers

Though lark buntings lack the colorful flair of other kinds of buntings, the bold black-and-white pattern of the males is still quite striking. Jacelyn refers to this species as the "fluttery birds," saying they "always fly just a little out of reach." Jacelyn points out that the striped brown female lark buntings look so different from the males that you may not even think they are the same species. She suggests looking for white wing patches when identifying females or male lark buntings during nonbreeding season.

Winter Wonders

Snow buntings, which are white with black accents, breed from coast to coast but only in the far north, from eastern Canada's Newfoundland and Labrador province all the way over to Alaska. In winter, they move south in great numbers. Some years they are spotted as far south as Oklahoma and Arkansas. Jacelyn says she most often encounters these cold-hardy fliers in roadside flocks.

"To me, snow buntings are quintessential during Christmas bird counts, even though we only track them down about half the time on our eastern Wyoming routes," she says.

Snow buntings occasionally gather to eat off the ground under feeders in a junco-like manner. Otherwise, look for them in open fields and roadside ditches, and along lakeshores.

Southern Lurkers

More widespread in Mexico, the varied bunting has a restricted range in the southwestern United States. Look for this bird in streamside habitats in the canyons along the borderlands. Breeding occurs in early summer in Texas. In Arizona, the nesting matches up to the rainy season in August.

Varied buntings look similar to indigos, but they are even more richly colored. Males can appear nearly purple with reddish highlights along the back of the head and on the throat. Females and young males are a soft gray-brown hue. Look for especially thick and curved bills on varieds, too.

Whether you're lucky enough to spot one at a backyard feeder or need to head to a nearby nature lookout, buntings are worthy of any birding life list.

Varied bunting

Snow bunting

A Woodpecker's World

From tree-climbing downies to ground-foraging flickers to sap-loving sapsuckers, woodpeckers delight and entertain us with their unique markings, fascinating flight patterns and distinctive drumming sounds. Here are fun facts to enrich your viewing of these dashing birds.

WOODS FOR WOODPECKERS

Most woodpecker species are tied to forests, woodlands and shrublands. Depending on the species, the fliers may prefer woodland edges (northern flicker), woodlands near water (downy woodpecker) or oak woodlands (acorn woodpecker), to name just a few.

Downy woodpecker

Northern
flicker

Strong, dense neck muscles
allow woodpeckers to
repeatedly drill up to
20 times a second, while
extra muscles in the skull
act as a protective helmet
by keeping the brain from
jiggling around when a
woodpecker is drumming.

▲ HIDEY HOLES

Usually, the bigger the woodpecker, the bigger the hole it makes. The nesting cavities of large pileated woodpeckers range from 10 to 24 inches deep, which is twice as deep as those of downy and red-bellied woodpeckers.

◀ THIRD LEG

Stiff tail feathers act as a brace, forming a tripod with the bird's feet to stabilize a woodpecker as it hops up a tree and chisels into the bark.

▼ SUPER HEARING

With strong hearing skills, woodpeckers listen for the sounds of insects crawling and chewing in the wood of a tree before using their strong, sharp bills to capture their prey.

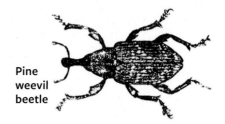

Pine
weevil
beetle

Northern flicker

Pileated

Downy

▲ CRAZY TONGUE

To reach deep into crevices in search of grubs, ants and sap, a woodpecker's tongue can be as long as up to a third of its total body length—so long that when it's retracted, it coils around the back of the bird's skull.

▶ GREAT AND SMALL

In North America, the downy is the smallest and most widespread woodpecker, while the pileated is the largest (except for the ivory-billed woodpecker, which experts consider to be most likely extinct).

▶ ROLLER COASTER RIDE

Woodpeckers fly in an undulating pattern similar to that of goldfinches. The pattern name comes from the Latin word *unda*, which means "wave." The motion has been compared to a roller coaster—the bird flaps its wings during the rising phase, then glides as it descends into the valley of the wave.

Red-naped sapsucker

Williamson's sapsucker females look nothing like the males, which are black. Males sport red throats, yellow bellies and white wing bars. The species is found in western mountain forests, where it may live in the same groves as red-naped and red-breasted sapsuckers.

▲ HOME SWEET HOME

Woodpeckers are primarily cavity nesters that excavate their own nest spots in dead or dying trees. The cavities will usually hold three to six eggs, and both parents tend the young birds. Woodpeckers sleep in cavities throughout the year.

▶ NIMBLE TOES

With four toes—the first and fourth facing backward, the second and third facing forward—woodpeckers can navigate up and around tree trunks. The scientific name for this toe arrangement is zygodactylism.

Flicker foot

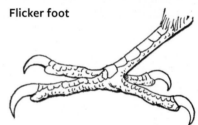

IN THE BARK

Some species pry off the outer layers of bark to expose insects and then drill into the softer bark beneath to look for insect larvae. This is called "bark sloughing."

▶ SNACK ATTACK

As omnivores, woodpeckers eat insects, spiders, seeds, nuts and acorns, as well as fruit and sap, and will even sip nectar from a hummingbird feeder on occasion. They also love suet, which you can provide in a hanging feeder cage to attract them to your yard.

Acorn Woodpecker

WANTED DEAD OR ALIVE

Woodpeckers prefer dead or dying trees because the trees are insect magnets and make drilling a nest easier. But the birds will also visit live trees, which may contain tree-dwelling or wood-boring insects.

The Gila woodpecker thrives in the nearly treeless desert habitats of the southwestern United States and Mexico. These woodpeckers excavate holes in living saguaro cactuses, allow the plants to dry out and then inhabit them.

DRILLING VERSUS DRUMMING

Woodpeckers use their sharp bills to drill into trees to find food or to make holes for nesting and roosting in spring and fall. Drumming, on the other hand, is most commonly done in spring to attract a mate or to mark territory by alerting the competition.

Black Beauties

Common grackles

Bright, colorful birds get all the glory, but these captivating coal-colored creatures are fun to encounter, even if some of them are a bit spooky looking

American
crow

BAD OMEN
Crows and their
larger cousins, the
ravens, are often
represented in
fables and folklore.
Seeing a single
crow is bad luck
in some cultures.

European
starling

Double-crested cormorant

MOVIE MADNESS
The Birds, a horror-thriller film released in 1963, made movie-goers fearful of feathered friends, especially those sporting midnight hues.

American Crow

These super smart, big birds are jet black from crown to claw, and they can be heard cawing across the continent. Crows are ground feeders and eat almost anything: carrion, chicks, small animals, seeds, insects, earthworms and more.

Trudy Stone, a backyard birder based in Nashville, Tennessee, respects crows for their intelligence. When she was young, Trudy's family had regular run-ins with crows, which used to collect her mom's Coppertone caps as she sat out sunbathing. "They'd steal the tops, and then they had a hidy-hole they'd put them in," she recalls.

American crows previously lived primarily in rural areas, but their habitat has changed over time. These clever creatures have used their smarts to adapt to life in cities, and are now common fixtures in urban birding.

Common Grackle

Look for glossy iridescent features on these long-tailed, beautiful blackbirds. Residing east of the Rocky Mountains, the ground feeders use their long legs to walk in lawns and fields, eating anything edible, from crops to food castoffs.

According to the Cornell Lab of Ornithology, common grackles are the top threat to corn, as they "eat ripening corn as well as corn sprouts, and their habit of foraging in big flocks mean they have a multimillion-dollar impact." That said, populations are in steep decline and have fallen an estimated 54% over the course of about 50 years.

European Starling

Also iridescent in plumage, European starlings are stocky songbirds that sport short tails, orange feet and long, bright yellow bills. Often found in cities and towns, these ground foragers eat insects.

In the 1890s, about 100 European starlings were brought across the Atlantic and released into New York City's Central Park. In that era, people introduced birds from all over the world to North America, but only a few species became established. Their population today is estimated at 200 million from Alaska to Mexico.

Adult male American redstart

Double-Crested Cormorant

With yellow-orange face accents, a snaky neck, aquamarine eyes and matte black plumage, these long, tall birds appear almost prehistoric. Birders find them across the country, often standing on docks or islands in fresh or salt water, stretching their wings to dry in the sun. These expert fishers are efficient hunters and are often in conflict with those who work in the aquaculture industry, including catfish farmers.

"Large flocks of cormorants come through, and they can wipe out a pond," says Greg Yarrow, one of the founders of the Internet Center for Wildlife Damage Management. "They've been deemed 'murder on wings' by some."

American Redstart

These coal black warblers sport striking orange plumage on their wings, tails and sides. Birders can spot these sweeties, found across the U.S., in deciduous woodlands, hopping along tree limbs or dashing through trees in search of insects. The birds are known for flashing their feathers to frighten their prey from out of the foliage. Redstarts are attracted to small fruits such as barberries, serviceberries and magnolia berries.

Black Vulture

A plentiful Southeast-based scavenger, the black vulture has a black body, a short tail, a wrinkly black head and white wingtips, which are visible as these birds soar the skies. "They are flying waste management," Greg says.

Long known as scavengers, vultures have evolved their feeding techniques over time and now are also considered predators. They regularly come into conflict with humans, damaging property and eating young livestock, so people have invented unique means of scaring this bird, which some consider spooky. "Use effigies of vultures and hang them upside down. This tends to freak the vultures out," Greg says.

Common Loon

Haunting, eerie calls are the hallmark of this fish-eating fowl. Spotted on lakes and ponds across the U.S., these black-and-white water birds are agile divers as well as strong swimmers. They chase, catch and grip fish with the frighteningly sharp projections on the roof of their mouth and tongue.

They come ashore only to nest, and they look much less intense on land. Their legs are at the back of their body for strong swimming, but it makes walking awkward.

SPOOKY SOUNDS
The haunting call of a common loon is frequently used as a sound effect during spooky scenes in many shows and movies, such as *Harry Potter, Game of Thrones* and *1917*.

Common loon

Black
vulture

CHAPTER 3

Backyard Bird Field Guide

Find out more about your feathered neighbors

Lesser
goldfinch

Guess the Goldfinch

Don't let the name fool you. The lesser goldfinch is just as special as its popular cousin.

Female lesser goldfinch

WHEN IT COMES to goldfinches, what does "lesser" mean, exactly? Is it a jab that compares the lesser goldfinch to the beautiful American goldfinch, as some birders joke? Emma Greig, project leader for the Cornell Lab of Ornithology's Project FeederWatch, shares the answer—and it has more to do with size than status. Simply put, "lesser goldfinches are a wee bit smaller than American goldfinches," Emma says.

The Tiniest of the Trio

Small in stature, goldfinches are songbirds with stubby cone-shaped bills. Their tails are short and notched, and their wings are long and pointed. The lesser goldfinch weighs about one-third of an ounce and is about 4 inches long. Lawrence's goldfinches are a bit bigger, while American goldfinches are heavier and top the charts at about 5 inches long.

Captivating in Color

Lesser goldfinches are known for olive green undertones. Males have yellow bellies and black caps. In the eastern part of their range, from Wyoming to Texas, they have black backs. Farther west, their backs are green. Females sport muted olive above and yellow below. Both sexes have a white patch on their wings.

Best in the West

In the United States, lesser goldfinches are most common in the Southwest, from California to Texas. A few can be found as far north as Washington and Wyoming, especially in summer. South of the United States, these adaptable little finches flutter over tropical habitats in Mexico, Central America and northwestern South America.

Peculiar Flight Patterns

It's possible to identify finches in flight simply by focusing on their flight patterns.

"Goldfinches undulate when they fly," Emma says. "They flap their wings and go up a little bit, then close their wings and go down a little bit." She says this could be a potential energy-saving strategy.

Beloved Mating Behaviors

In spring, listen for the light twittering from the treetops as lesser goldfinches meet their mates. A courting pair looks and chirps at each other before forming a bond and preparing a nest in a scrub oak, cottonwood or willow tree. And they show their appreciation in small, sweet ways. "Males provide food to the females during courtship and also while the females are incubating eggs," Emma says.

> "Lesser goldfinches frequently visit my yard and sit in my pinyon pine tree. I love to watch them from my porch."
>
> **Lisa Fisher**
> CARSON CITY, NEVADA

HAPPY AND THRIVING

While many bird populations are declining, lesser goldfinch numbers have increased over the past 50 years. "They really thrive in habitat that is modified by people, such as scrubby areas, backyards, parks and fields," says Emma Greig of the Cornell Lab of Ornithology.

FEEDERS AND PLANTS

Lure goldfinches with Nyjer or black oil sunflower seeds. Or plant thistle if you have the space. Goldfinches are among the few species that feed seeds to their nestlings, and they'll do so with planted thistle.

WATER FEATURES
Birdbaths draw warblers for a clean drink and quick dip. Use a water wiggler or a solar fountain to tempt birds while keeping mosquitoes at bay.

Hairy woodpecker

CONSERVE SUET
Feed more fliers and fewer squirrels with a suet saver feeder equipped with an insert to prevent pests.

Welcome Warblers

Decode the secret ways to lure these springtime visitors to your landscape

BACKYARD REGULARS, such as cardinals and finches, love to dine on seeds. But warblers, cherished arrivals in the spring, tend to avoid feeders.

"Most warblers are insectivorous and won't eat seeds," says Emma Greig, project leader for the Cornell Lab of Ornithology's Project FeederWatch. "Many warbler species glean insects from treetops and dense foliage, so they aren't interested in an exposed feeder."

Noteworthy Visitors
Some exceptions exist, though. "Fortunately, a few species are brave enough to visit suet feeders," says Emma. She notes that the yellow-throated warbler is a special visitor in the Southeast.

Its distinctive black, gray and white coloring, combined with a vivid sunny chin, makes this bird a real treat to spot.

Yellow-rumped warblers also have splashes of yellow, mainly at the sides of the chest and above the tail feathers. These warblers are widespread in the U.S. and sometimes visit seed as well as suet feeders. In the East, they may form mixed flocks with brownish yellow pine warblers, a species that also enjoys suet and seeds.

Wide-ranging orange-crowned warblers also stop by feeders. They are a somewhat drab olive yellow with an orange head patch that is typically hard to spot, but they're fun to watch as they puncture flowers to drain the nectar. They will also check out hummingbird feeders at times.

Out west, Townsend's warblers, with their yellow-and-black-striped heads, show similar behaviors. They especially love to drink from flowers during spring migration and may drop by a mealworm or sugar-water feeder.

Seasonal Suet
Winter and early spring are the ideal times to attract warblers. "Suet is best offered in cooler weather so it won't melt or go rancid," says Emma. "That's also when warblers need an extra boost, since insects aren't readily available."

Try to look for high-quality suet cakes with mealworms and choose no-melt versions if spring is warm in your area.

Helpful Habitats
Feeders aren't the only way to entice warblers. "Trees, shrubs and native plants that promote healthy insect populations are the perfect way to support warblers," Emma says. "Don't use pesticides in your yard. The more insects around, the better."

Yellow-throated warblers, such as this male, are special visitors at suet feeders.

Cardinal Clues

Take a closer look at one of the backyard's most iconic birds

Northern cardinal

8 Young cardinals are demanding. In the first days after they hatch, their parents feed them up to eight times an hour.

3 It takes three to nine days for a cardinal pair to build a nest, with the female doing most of the work.

2 Northern cardinals fiercely defend their territories. Two pro sports teams (the NFL's Arizona Cardinals and MLB's St. Louis Cardinals) are named for this bird and its fighting spirit.

20 While most pairs mate for several breeding seasons, about 20% break up each year.

16 Ornithologists have identified 16 distinct cardinal calls.

1918

Before the Migratory Bird Treaty Act of 1918, it was legal to keep wild birds as pets. Northern cardinals were a popular choice.

MELANISTIC

Melanistic common pheasant

Albino American crow

ALBINO

Most animals—including humans—produce melanin, which pigments hair, skin and more. In birds, it's responsible for black, brown and tan feathers. When a visitor is melanistic, it will appear much darker than normal.

An albino bird lacks all melanin. It sports completely white plumage and is usually devoid of any regular field marks, making it tricky to identify. Look past the feathers to tell a true albino—the eyes, beak and legs are always red or pink.

Imperfect Plumage

Four rare genetic traits that affect feather colors

Leucistic hummingbird

LEUCISTIC

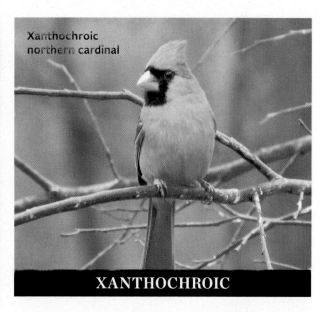

Xanthochroic northern cardinal

XANTHOCHROIC

Leucistic birds have incredibly varied patterns. They may appear more muted than their counterparts or they can be dotted with white patches. These birds are occasionally mistaken for albinos, but leucistic birds always have some pigment in their feathers or on other body parts, such as their feet, eyes or beak.

If a bird is yellow or orange where red feathers should be, it could have xanthochroism. Unlike the other conditions covered here, this one can be caused by diet or genetics. It's more obvious in birds with lots of red plumage, including cardinals and male house finches.

Blue jay

Westward Ho!

Blue jays are fixtures in the East, but these adaptive birds are on the move

WITH ITS DISTINCT blue and white plumage, black necklace and pointed crest, a blue jay is hard to miss. Feisty, loud and intelligent members of the corvid family, blue jays are taking center stage in more western backyards.

Follow the Food

Traditionally at home in eastern deciduous forests, blue jays feed on both seeds and insects. While they thrive on acorns, their versatile diet allows them to easily expand their territory to new habitats.

As more people moved west, they planted trees and put up bird feeders, creating ecological stepping stones, according to Tim Meehan, a quantitative ecologist for the National Audubon Society. "Blue jays started hopping from one yard to the next," he says.

Tim says, after looking at more than a century of data collected during the Christmas Bird Count, blue jays started to appear in the western regions by the 1960s. They're now full-time residents in many of these areas, with reports of them venturing to the coast and as far north as Washington and British Columbia.

Leaving Home

Often mating for life, blue jay pairs build their nests 10 to 25 feet high in the outer branches of trees. The birds are highly territorial and will dive-bomb anything entering their domain they may consider a threat.

"They're all over Boulder, Colorado, during the breeding season from March to August," says Tim about his hometown. "After that, there's pressure on the youngsters to go find their own habitat." This behavior causes the jay's range to slowly expand.

"In the winter, you see a similar pattern," says Tim. Blue jays do not migrate long distances as other songbirds do. But in some areas, such as the Canadian provinces, they'll move south. They often remain in areas with mild winters. Tim adds, "They move only when there's good reason to."

The good news is that the birds' movements do not appear to affect other members of the corvid family that are already established in the West. Because blue jays occupy a different type of habitat, they fill an empty niche.

Blue Jay Buffet

To encourage backyard blue jays, install feeding platforms near shrubs for cover. Stock the platforms with peanuts, fruit, sunflower seeds and mealworms. Suet feeders are also a hit.

It's equally beneficial to include trees, such as American beech or native oak trees, in your landscape to provide a supply of food and a safe place to nest. Birdbaths are always well received, particularly in regions with little rain.

"I have blue jays all year. Recently, I put up a feeder and a whole family decided that it was the place to eat. It was so much fun to watch the juveniles learn the family pecking order."

Bob Krouse
MACKINAW, ILLINOIS

ALL-AROUND APPEAL

Platform feeders attract a variety of birds. A recycled plastic tray feeder is large enough to accommodate blue jays and has a mesh bottom to keep seed dry.

Juvenile yellow-bellied
sapsucker

SQUEAKY SOUNDS

Yellow-bellied sapsucker calls
are a repeated series of nasally
mewing sounds. Licia Kuckkahn
Johnson says the noise
resembles a raspy, squeaky
dog toy being chewed on
over and over.

TOP TREES

*Sapsuckers visit hundreds
of trees, but here are some
of their favorites:*

Aspen
Eastern hemlock
Elm
Paper birch
Red hickory
Sugar maple
Yellow birch

Elm

Sap Tappers

Listen for drumming as the yellow-bellied
sapsucker looks for sweet treats in the trees

SAPSUCKERS ARE A group of
specialized woodpeckers that tap
out row after row of individual sap
wells in tree trunks. The yellow-
bellied sapsucker is seen in the
eastern half of the U.S. and across
the northern forests, while the
red-naped, Williamson's and
red-breasted are in the West.

Licia Kuckkahn Johnson,
education director and naturalist
at the North Lakeland Discovery
Center in Manitowish Waters,
Wisconsin, remembers seeing
her first yellow-bellied sapsucker
and thinking that it didn't look
very yellow to her. But she was
particularly excited when she was
able to identify their sap wells for
the first time.

"After 20 years of teaching, I still
love asking folks what they think
made those crazy patterns on the
trees," she says.

Standing Out

Vertical white wing patches
distinguish yellow-bellieds from
similar black-and-white downy and
hairy woodpeckers. According to
Licia, the full red forehead helps
with identification too. She also
says, "If a bird has a red throat, you
know right away it is a male, and if
the throat is white, you are looking
at a female sapsucker."

Young yellow-bellieds have a
brownish coloration, but their
white wing patches, like those of
the adults, are still a useful field
mark to look for.

On the Move

These sapsuckers are migratory,
which is rare for woodpeckers.
They live in a variety of habitats,
from low-lying flood plains to
mountainous forests at 10,000 feet.

Their breeding range extends
from Alaska to Newfoundland, and
south along the Appalachians. They
winter across the East, from New
Jersey west to Texas and all the
way south to Panama.

Male yellow-bellied sapsuckers
drum out slow Morse code-like
territory notes. A common breeding
display involves males pointing
their bills skyward as they showcase
their red throat patch for an
interested female. Though both
sexes are involved with excavating
nesting cavities, males maintain
most of the workload.

Sweet Snacks

Yellow-bellied sapsuckers often
feed from trees in young deciduous
or mixed forest stands. During
the springtime, flowing sap
wells provide nourishment to the
sapsuckers as well as insects, bats
and other birds, including ruby-
throated hummingbirds.

Sapsuckers also snack on insects
they glean from tree trunks or catch
out of the air. Native berries round
out the bird's diet, and yellow-
bellieds will occasionally stop by
for suet. Consider growing fruit-
producing plants, and keep an eye
on your suet feeder to see if the
birds visit your backyard.

Male
yellow-bellied
sapsucker

Barn Swallow Stats

Discover what makes this fork-tailed flier so special

Barn swallow

850
Some experts suggest a barn swallow can gobble up to 850 bugs a day.

100
These birds are commonly seen swooping low over fields or water, eating their food on the go. But they are also known to look for prey up to 100 feet in the air.

1876
George Grinnell became editor of *Forest and Stream* magazine in 1876 and later launched a campaign to stop barn swallows and egrets from being hunted for hat feathers.

6 Barn swallows are found on six continents: North and South America, Europe, Africa, Asia and Australia.

5,000
Traditionally, British sailors would get a barn swallow tattoo after traveling 5,000 nautical miles. The bird symbolized the hope of the sailor returning home or to a loved one.

4-5
Male and female barn swallow pairs each build a cup nest together, using mud and dried grass. A nest holds four to five eggs on average.

Bald eagle

EAGLES

Red-tailed hawk

HAWKS

North America is home to two species of eagles: bald and golden. Check out their expansive wings and their ability to soar. They're hunters and scavengers, feeding on fish, small animals and carrion.

LOOK FOR:

Extremely large wingspans, up to 7 feet or more, for both species.

A large and diverse group, many hawks (especially Cooper's and red-taileds) are widespread across the U.S. and are comfortable visiting backyards in search of a meal.

LOOK FOR:

The rounded shape of the wings and tails on these birds, along with stout bodies.

Raptor Roll Call

Take a closer look at common types of birds of prey

American kestrel

FALCONS

Osprey

OSPREY

These birds have a need for speed; some species can exceed 200 mph in flight. Falcons come in a variety of sizes—the tiny American kestrel is only 10 inches long.

LOOK FOR:

An extra-long hook in their beaks, known as a tomial tooth, used to rip their food.

Ospreys are classified in a different family from all other raptors. Often mistaken for bald eagles because of their size and coloring, they eat solely live fish.

LOOK FOR:

Feet-first dives into water in pursuit of food, sometimes even fully submerging themselves.

PERFECT PAIR

The thorns of the huisache tree, also called a sweet acacia tree, provide protection for the verdin, while the yellow circular flower heads offer a backdrop that mirrors the bird's bright head.

At Home in the Desert

Find and attract verdins in southwestern scrubland settings

A juvenile verdin sports an all-gray look and a bright yellow beak that dulls over time.

VERDINS ARE THE tiny gray birds of the brush habitats from southern Utah and southwestern Oklahoma to central Mexico. Despite being relatively common and active, this energetic species can sometimes be easy to miss.

"Their coloration is so generally cryptic that it feels like a treat to spot one hopping about in the branches—and to get to see the yellow color on its head or the rust color on its shoulder," says Jennie Duberstein, coordinator for the Sonoran Joint Venture.

Dine and Dash

Verdins dine mostly on insects. To attract the birds, Jennie has a few recommendations. "Focus on providing verdins the plants and trees with the structures and food sources they need," she says. "In my yard they love the mesquite and paloverde trees, and they are also fans of cactus like chollas."

These spunky fliers often visit hummingbird feeders and nectar plants. Agile verdins can even eat while hanging upside down.

Constructing Cavities

Verdins construct incredible round abodes all year long, using some for nesting and others for roosting. Their homes are typically about 6 inches wide with an opening situated toward the bottom.

"These thorny globes are all-purpose houses, providing great protection from predators and extreme temperatures," Jennie says. Verdins' domed homes stay cooler in the summer and warmer in the winter.

Whistling Notes

Until she learned to recognize their three-note whistle, Jennie didn't realize how ubiquitous verdins were in her region. "Once I had it imprinted on my brain, I realized they were everywhere even if I couldn't immediately see them," she says.

Whenever she hears verdins now, Jennie looks to the trees and tries to spot them. Males do much of the singing, but during the breeding season females will occasionally sing back.

Support Verdins

While verdins are still common, between 1968 and 2015 their population declined 60% in North America. This rate of decline is alarming for Jennie, who didn't grow up in the Southwest and says it's a daily thrill to see verdins now.

The species is particularly vulnerable to habitat loss. One threat is buffelgrass (*Pennisetum ciliare*), an invasive grass that is altering fire patterns throughout much of the bird's range.

By supplying plants that verdins rely on—and by protecting Sonoran habitats—we can all help ensure that this spirited desert specialist continues to thrive.

"I spotted this young verdin on an early morning walk. I was happy it stayed around long enough for me to get a few pictures and to enjoy its beauty."

Caroline Horowitz
CHANDLER, ARIZONA

HELPING OUT

Male verdins stay involved and play a critical role in nest construction. The males mostly set up the thorny outer structures. Females handle the interior decorating, adding a soft lining that's usually a combo of grass and plant fibers.

LISTEN UP

The male verdin's song is a simple *tseet tsor tsor* whistle. Males and females both give a loud chip call, sometimes in a rapid progression.

**Male and female
rose-breasted grosbeaks**

"I have fed orioles for years but had an awesome surprise the day I took this photo. I was thrilled when rose-breasted grosbeaks showed up."

Pam Garcia
MANSFIELD, LOUISIANA

FLIMSY FLOORING

Rose-breasted grosbeaks build their nests so loosely that the three to five pale green to bluish eggs they lay can occasionally be spotted through the bottom.

TANTALIZING TREATS

Attract rose-breasted grosbeaks with these plants:

American elderberry

Arrowwood viburnum

Elms

Red mulberry

Serviceberry

Sunflowers

Virginia creeper

Winter's Festive Finch

Use sunflower seeds to lure these ruby red birds to your feeders

PURPLE FINCHES are an absolute backyard treat. Despite their name, they have a hue that's more reddish than purple. Roger Tory Peterson, the ornithologist and editor of the *Peterson Field Guide* series, once described these birds as a "sparrow dipped in raspberry juice."

These forest-dwelling songbirds are found mainly in the Midwest, in the East and along the Pacific Coast. Look for a bird that is slightly larger than a chickadee or nuthatch, with a short notched tail and a prominent, strong beak, which it mainly uses to crack into tough seeds.

Purple finches are often confused with house finches, but purples are heavier with shorter tails and longer wingtips. Male purple finches have an almost completely red face and neck, with pinkish red covering most of the body. Purple and house finches don't flock together, but they might show up at your feeder at the same time. In the West, Cassin's finches are also similarly colored. They have a bright red cap, like the purple, but a lighter pink face, neck and upper chest.

A musical bird, the purple finch sometimes copies other birds, such as American goldfinches or eastern towhees, as they sing loudly from the treetops. But when it's time to woo a mate, the male purple finch mellows his tune, hopping in front of the female and puffing his feathers. If she seems interested, the avian Romeo pops a foot in the air, vibrates his wings, and lands to present a twig or piece of grass.

Purples like to nest on the limbs of conifers, though in the southern part of their breeding range they might nest in an oak, maple or cherry tree. The female carefully builds a twig cup, about 7 inches across and 4 inches deep, lining it with grass, moss and animal fur in preparation for the young.

Clutches range from two to seven eggs, pale green with brown and black marks, each just under an inch long. It takes less than two weeks for the eggs to hatch. Afterward, both parents feed the naked, helpless chicks. The young grow quickly and fledge in two weeks.

Don't worry if finches visited your backyard last winter but don't show up this year. They migrate erratically. Those that breed in Canada head to the central and southern United States for the winter, while the ones that spend their summer on the Pacific Coast, around the Great Lakes and in the Northeast often don't migrate at all, except to lower elevations.

They'll probably be back again, especially if your feeders are filled with black oil sunflower seeds—a finch favorite.

**Male rose-breasted
grosbeak**

CHAPTER 4

Amazing Hummingbirds

Learn all about the unique traits of these avian superstars

Black-chinned
hummingbird

FASTEST
WINGBEAT

LIGHTEST WEIGHT

MOST
EFFICIENT
METABOLISM

QUICKEST
HEARTBEAT

SMALLEST
EGGS

Mini Marvels

Hummingbirds have traits that make them entertaining, but those
same qualities help them thrive

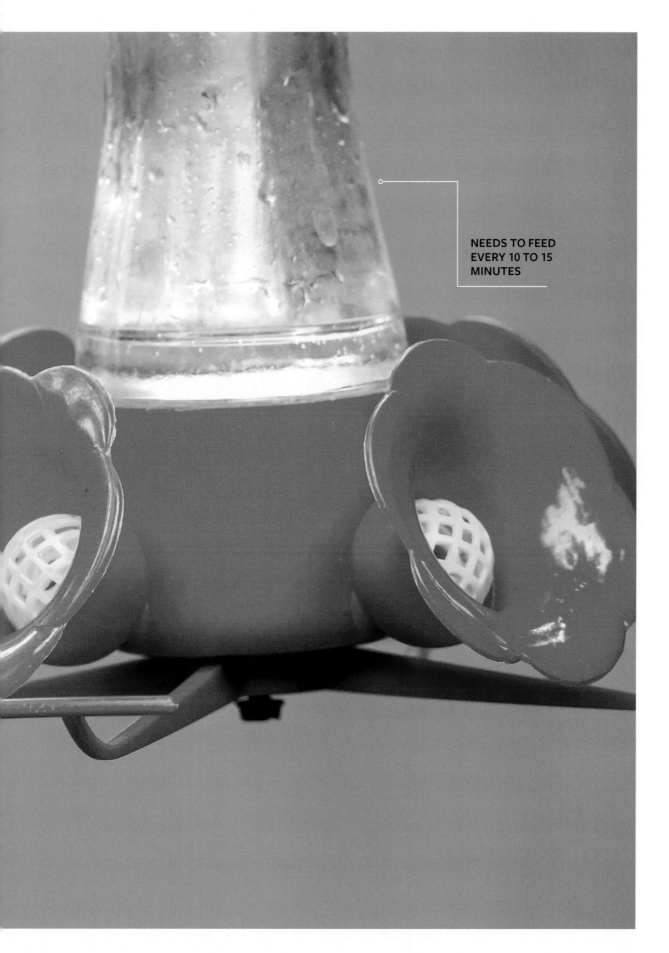

NEEDS TO FEED
EVERY 10 TO 15
MINUTES

50 OR MORE
WINGBEATS
PER SECOND

Rufous
hummingbird

WEIGHS
3 TO 4
GRAMS

Ruby-throated
hummingbird

SMALL BUT SPEEDY. Tiny but aggressive. Little bodies, big appetites. Hummingbirds are a study in extremes. They are the lightest North American birds. Most weigh less than two pennies at 3 to 4 grams. They have the fastest wings and heartbeats, the most efficient metabolisms, and the most minuscule eggs. The list could go on.

But hummingbirds are tough survivalists. Many of the actions that help them persevere also make them fun to watch. Here are amazing hummingbird traits and behaviors you might witness and the biological reasons behind them.

Whirring Feathers

Soon after Chris Clark, an associate professor at the University of California, Riverside, began studying Anna's hummingbirds, he wondered about their tails. "They're these little fighter jets," he says. "What are they doing evolving these really long tails that might slow them down?" He discovered in his research that the stiff tail feathers of male Anna's make songlike sounds. These noises are part of the courtship display as the males dive to attract females' favor.

The wings of hummingbirds make different sounds—what Chris calls wing trills. "On broadtailed hummingbirds, the males have this little notch in the outer part of their wings," he says. "They sound like a cricket when they fly."

Other species, including Allen's, rufous, and to a lesser extent ruby-throated and black-chinned, also have these trills. And in these birds, the trills are in place of songs, Chris says, with males using the sounds to declare and defend territory.

Extreme Speed

A hummingbird's namesake hum is created by air moving around its wings as they beat over 50 times per second. But it's not the speed of its wings that allows a hummingbird to hover—it's the structure of its wing joints. Hummingbirds can rotate their wings as they flap. This lifts them into the air on both the forward and backward strokes. They're also among the fastest fliers for their size, reaching speeds of up to 37 mph, and up to 60 mph in courtship dives.

An Instinct to Protect

Despite their tiny size, hummingbirds are fierce—they will chase almost any intruder from the feeders or flowers they're protecting. "Birds that drink nectar tend to be aggressive," Chris says. Researchers' best hypothesis: Most birds need to find their food—hidden seeds or grubs—but hummingbirds feed on flowers that are showy by nature. That means the birds can see all their food sources, but so does the competition. "They evolved to be really aggressive defending that food from other animals that might also eat it."

Olympic Metabolisms

Hummingbirds actively defend their food sources because they need to feed every 10 to 15 minutes. Flying is an energy-intense endeavor for hummers. In the process, they ingest levels of sugar that would be dangerous to other animals. That's what led Ken Welch Jr., an associate professor at the University of Toronto Scarborough, to study hummingbird metabolism. "Hummingbirds maintain a blood-sugar level, even when they're fasting, that would make your primary care physician falter," Ken says.

Hummingbirds have highly efficient digestive organs. The sugar gets into their bloodstream quickly, Ken says. "The average hovering metabolic rate of an Anna's hummingbird is, gram per gram, about 10 times what an elite human endurance athlete can achieve."

And that extremely fast metabolism also can plummet when the birds go into torpor to conserve energy or bulk up before migration. "They can go from the highest metabolic rate of any bird while hovering, to one of the lowest in torpor," Ken says. A study in biological extremes, indeed.

SWIVELING WINGS FOR MORE LIFT

Black-chinned hummingbird

FROZEN IN TIME

In August 1947, *National Geographic* published a series of photographs by Harold Edgerton of a ruby-throated hummingbird frozen in flight. The photos represented two groundbreaking inventions important to our appreciation of hummingbirds today.

The first was the creation of the electric flash, which could emit a burst of light that lasted 1/100,000 of a second. That made it possible to capture images our eyes couldn't see, including a hovering hummingbird's wings. This allowed bird enthusiasts to appreciate these tiny dynamos in detail previously unseen.

The second invention was the feeder that attracted the attention of that ruby-throated hummingbird. It was a blown-glass sugar-water feeder devised by Laurence Webster, who made it to feed hummingbirds in his New England gardens. *National Geographic* readers were immediately transfixed by the concept of feeding hummingbirds and wanted feeders of their own. In 1950 Audubon Novelty Company released the first commercially available hummingbird feeder and called it the Webster Hanging Feeder.

Defending Their Turf

Why hummingbirds guard their territories so fiercely

Two rufous hummingbirds square off.

A HUMMINGBIRD IS A WONDER to behold as it dances in the air to sip sweet nectar from flowers. You might imagine that such a delicate lover of sweetness would be among the most peaceful creatures in the world.

In reality, whenever two or more hummingbirds are present, things can get a little tense. The feisty birds zoom about, sparring in midair or chasing each other with chattering cries—relentless in their desire to defend their spaces.

Pollinator Contract

Hummingbirds, butterflies, bees and other pollinators each have a relationship with flowers that benefits both sides. Flowers produce nectar, which is rich in sugar, to attract these creatures. In turn, the birds and insects pick up pollen from one flower and carry it to another, helping the plant to reproduce.

But each bloom produces only a small amount of nectar at a time. If a hummingbird finds a group of flowers, it may visit them one at a time, taking sips from each while waiting for the others to replenish. A good flower patch might keep a hummingbird supplied with food all day—but only as long as the hummer can keep other fliers away.

When a hummingbird finds a stand of wildflowers or a blooming tree or vine, it may be easier for the hummer to defend the plant against competitors than to find another nectar source. So these birds have an instinct to quickly start protecting a feeding territory around the nectar supply they've discovered. It's likely to be only temporary, and the hummingbird may soon shift to another spot, but the instinct to guard a food source is always there.

Space out sugar-water feeders to prevent potential hummingbird confrontations.

Sugar-Water Showdown

A hummingbird's territorial instinct is so strong that it often carries over to situations where it's not as needed—for example, at hummingbird feeders with an endless supply of sugar water. No matter how often you refill your feeder, the hummingbirds don't realize that they don't have to fight over it. One aggressive individual may try to dominate a whole row of feeders, zooming in to drive away every other bird.

The best solution is to put your sugar-water feeders farther apart, so that one bird can't control them all. Or better yet, put the feeders out of sight of each other, perhaps on different sides of your house or in spots separated by trees. If that isn't possible, you may have an overly pushy solo hummingbird controlling your feeders until it decides to move on.

Pursuing a Mate

In the breeding season, a male hummingbird establishes a different kind of territory. He surveys his surroundings from a high perch. If another male shows up, he'll chase it away. If a female appears, he'll start putting on his special courtship display—often performing aerial acrobatics, with loud whirring or whistling sounds—to catch her attention.

If they mate, though, that's the end of their relationship, and he goes back to watching for more females. When the female builds her nest, it may or may not be in his territory. In the meantime, she'll defend a small territory of her own, chasing away other females that come too close to her nest.

Hummingbirds are a joy to watch, and they become even more fascinating when we understand the reasons behind some of their actions. You may get to observe these territorial behaviors in your own backyard.

ON GUARD

Many birds have specific ways of keeping potential intruders out of their claimed spaces

- Carolina wren pairs stay together to defend a permanent territory with songs and calls year-round.

- A male red-winged blackbird sings to announce a domain in the marsh for himself and his multiple mates, but only in the breeding season.

- Belted kingfishers protect feeding areas along rivers, chasing away other kingfishers that approach.

Hummingbird Tales

With so much to love about hummingbirds, spotting them out in nature is always a thrill. Take in these extraordinary moments that talented *Birds & Blooms* readers captured on camera.

Hummingbirds usually aren't deterred by rain. If flying in heavy rain, they'll speed up their wingbeats.

◀ **Each evening** during our vacation in Ridgedale, Missouri, a female ruby-throated hummingbird passed through the branches of a tree just off our porch. I brought my camera out one night in anticipation of her arrival. The light and the lovely bird were amazing and the blooms looked so much like fireworks.

Edward McFadden
MINNEAPOLIS, MINNESOTA

▲ **I took a picture** of a young male Costa's hummingbird in early January 2019 after a winter rain. It had snowed the week before, and I'd seen him on the same flower when it was covered in snow. But on this day, he perched there for the longest time and seemed to enjoy the rain.

Laura Stafford
TUCSON, ARIZONA

Male ruby-throats show off their red gorgets (the bright patches of throat feathers) when trying to attract a potential mate.

A male ruby-throated hummingbird would perch right outside of my laundry room window. I set up a Nikon D7200 camera with a Nikkor 600 mm prime lens inside on a rainy afternoon, opened the window and waited for him to rest on a branch. He was just about to take flight, heading toward an approaching female that would sometimes join him on the same branch.

Denise Hilley
SEVIERVILLE, TENNESSEE

▶ **I discovered an** Anna's hummingbird nest in one of the trees near my house. The nest was above eye level, so I didn't notice it until the babies were about a week and a half old. I set up a post about 10 feet away to take their pictures when they started becoming more active. After many attempts, I took this. About four days later, the first baby flew out of the nest.

Monica Slack
EL CAJON, CALIFORNIA

▼ **While on my farm,** I captured a beautiful ruby-throated hummingbird dancing among the sunflowers as it sipped the sweet nectar. Sunflowers and hummingbirds always bring a smile to my face.

Martha Tully
GLEN SPEY, NEW YORK

Attract hummingbirds with a mister or fountain, which gives them an opportunity to rinse off their feathers and beaks.

▲ **It was a very** warm April a few years ago, so our birdbath went out a bit early. Almost immediately this Anna's hummingbird began splashing around. It went from pool to pool on the waterfall and seemed to enjoy washing its beak. May was cooler, but the bird still visited the waterfall from time to time.

Reg Robazza
SURREY, BRITISH COLUMBIA

▶ **I call this shot** *The Glowing Hummingbird*. I was at a local wildlife management area to photograph hummingbirds. When I took the shot, I knew the sun was in a good location to highlight the colors of the Mexican sunflower and the ruby-throated hummingbird. But I did not think it would light up the bird the way it did!

William Friggle
DENVER, PENNSYLVANIA

This photo is special because the ruby-throated hummingbird and monarch butterfly are so close together in a group of dahlias. I shot the photo with a Canon EOS 7D Mark II camera and a Canon EF 400 mm lens.

Richard A. Schultz
WAUSAU, WISCONSIN

Living in Las Vegas,
I'm lucky enough to see hummingbirds in my backyard year-round. This particular Anna's hummingbird perched on a branch and struck a pose as though it knew that it was born to be on camera. I snapped the photo with a Canon EOS Rebel T2i camera.

Jodi Zimmerman
LAS VEGAS, NEVADA

► Ruby-throated hummingbirds really enjoy the potted hibiscus in my backyard. I love the size comparison between the flower and the tiny hummingbird in this photo. To capture the wings in action, I used a shutter speed of 1/3200.

Renee Annis
CHESNEE, SOUTH CAROLINA

▼ This rare visitor stopped by a backyard in Millersburg, Ohio, in late fall. The property owner, Martha, was kind enough to allow me and many others to see her unexpected guest, a male rufous hummingbird. He stayed well into November, and Martha made sure his food didn't freeze.

Matthew Montonini
MENTOR, OHIO

Rufous hummingbirds sometimes stray into the eastern half of the U.S. during their fall migration.

Rufous
hummingbird at
honeysuckle vine

Hummingbird Highways

Learn about the epic migratory feats
of these tiny garden favorites

Ruby-throated hummingbird at hibiscus

Ruby-throated at a sugar-water feeder

IT SEEMS ALMOST IMPOSSIBLE that a hummingbird could even exist. A bird no bigger than a large beetle, covered with feathers that glow and sparkle in the sun, it hovers on wings that beat more than 50 times per second, dancing in front of flowers to sip sweet nectar. That would make it remarkable enough. But on top of that, some hummingbirds migrate long distances—hundreds or even thousands of miles—leaving cold climates for the winter and returning in the spring. Read on for insights into how they accomplish these amazing travels.

Traveling Traits

Many kinds of birds, from geese to goldfinches, typically migrate in flocks. But hummingbirds travel as loners—each individual navigates on its own. Even young birds making their first southward migration fly solo, without any guidance from their parents. Instead, they rely on instinct.

Hummingbirds have a rapid metabolism, burning energy quickly, so they frequently stop to feed as they travel. Any time they come to a good patch of flowers or feeders, they pause and spend some time tanking up. During peak migration periods, food sources may be swarming with hummers zooming around and sparring in midair as they compete for nectar. At such concentration points, they arrive and leave singly, not in flocks. Each individual's journey is a series of relatively short flights punctuated by refueling stops.

While most songbirds and some other kinds of birds migrate mainly at night, hummingbirds travel mostly in the daytime, flying fairly low—taking advantage of the warm sunlight and watching carefully for flowers or feeders along the way.

Schedule and Route

The timing of a hummingbird's migration and the route that it takes are dictated mostly by instincts rather than by conscious choices. But those instincts have developed over many years based on what has worked best for the survival of previous generations.

In spring, when hummers are moving north toward their breeding grounds, they have no way of knowing what the weather is like up ahead. Their instincts guide them to arrive at each stop along the way on dates when, in an average year, the coldest weather has passed and some flowers have started blooming. In late summer or fall, when hummers start to move south, they aren't driven out by bad weather or lack of food. In fact, they usually leave while food is still abundant.

In eastern North America, migrating hummingbirds may follow the same general routes in spring and fall, simply reversing directions with the season. In the West, the many mountain ranges—with strikingly different weather at different elevations—make travel more complicated, and many hummers follow very different routes while traveling to and from their breeding grounds.

Of course, many tropical hummingbirds are nonmigratory, because their habitats provide a good living all year. Even in North America, some are permanent residents. All along the Pacific Coast, some Anna's hummingbirds stay in the same places year-round, while other species are present only during the warmer half of the year.

Anna's hummingbird

Ruby-Throated Migration

As the only hummingbirds nesting east of the Great Plains, ruby-throats do a stellar job of representing the family. In summer they are found almost throughout the eastern United States and southeastern Canada. During the coldest months, a few stay in the southeastern states, but the vast majority migrate to a winter range that stretches from southern Mexico to Panama. For many, their summer and winter homes are more than 2,000 miles apart.

Adult male ruby-throats are on the move by late July and early August; most female and young ruby-throats start moving two to four weeks later. Large numbers move south along the Texas coast in mid-September, and most arrive in Costa Rica in October or early November. In spring, adult males may move north from the tropics by late February. The peak arrival of ruby-throats in the southeastern states is mid-to-late April, and most don't show up in the Northeast until around the beginning of May.

To accomplish the epic journey, most ruby-throated hummingbirds don't fly straight north and south. Instead, many move toward the southwest in fall and toward the northeast in spring. Why? Because most are detouring around the Gulf of Mexico. Experts think that some fly straight across the Gulf, a journey of at least 600 miles that could take 18 hours or more, but scientists still don't know what percentage of the population might do that.

Ruby-throated with nestlings

The Rufous Routes

A dozen species of western hummingbirds are at least partly migratory, but the rufous is the long-distance champion. Its main winter range is in southwestern Mexico, and in summer some reach southern Alaska—so individuals may travel almost 4,000 miles one way in spring and fall.

Ruby-throated at feeder

WHEN TO TAKE DOWN FEEDERS

Backyard birders often wonder if keeping a hummingbird feeder up in fall will stop the birds from leaving. The answer is no. Instincts drive the timing of hummers' migration, not the availability of food. When it's time for them to head toward their wintering grounds, they fly away from gardens filled with flowers and feeders. Rarely, a stray hummingbird stays far north in a snowy climate in winter, visiting a heated feeder. But that's due to faulty instincts—the feeder didn't keep the bird from going where it should have gone.

Their journey looks unusual on both the calendar and the map. Instead of moving north in spring and south in fall, they move northwest in late winter and southeast in late summer. Some adult males may leave their wintering grounds in January, since they start to show up in the western United States in February. Rufous hummingbirds travel northwest along the coast and through the lowland deserts, where flowers can be abundant at that season.

By the middle of May they have occupied almost all of their breeding range, which stretches from the northwestern states through western Canada to southern Alaska. Adult males may leave their breeding territories by mid-June, beginning to move east and southeast through mountainous regions. High mountain meadows that had been snow-covered in spring will be filled with flowers by July and August, and rufous hummingbirds swarm there throughout late summer, gradually making their way back toward Mexico.

Maybe because so many rufous hummingbirds start their southward migration by moving east, they are especially likely to wander to the eastern states in fall. Some have shifted their migratory behavior, and hundreds now spend winters in gardens across the southeastern states, establishing a new migratory route that didn't exist just a few years ago. That hummingbirds can change to a completely new destination is just one more fascinating thing about these tiny but tremendous travelers.

Rufous hummingbird on sugar sumac

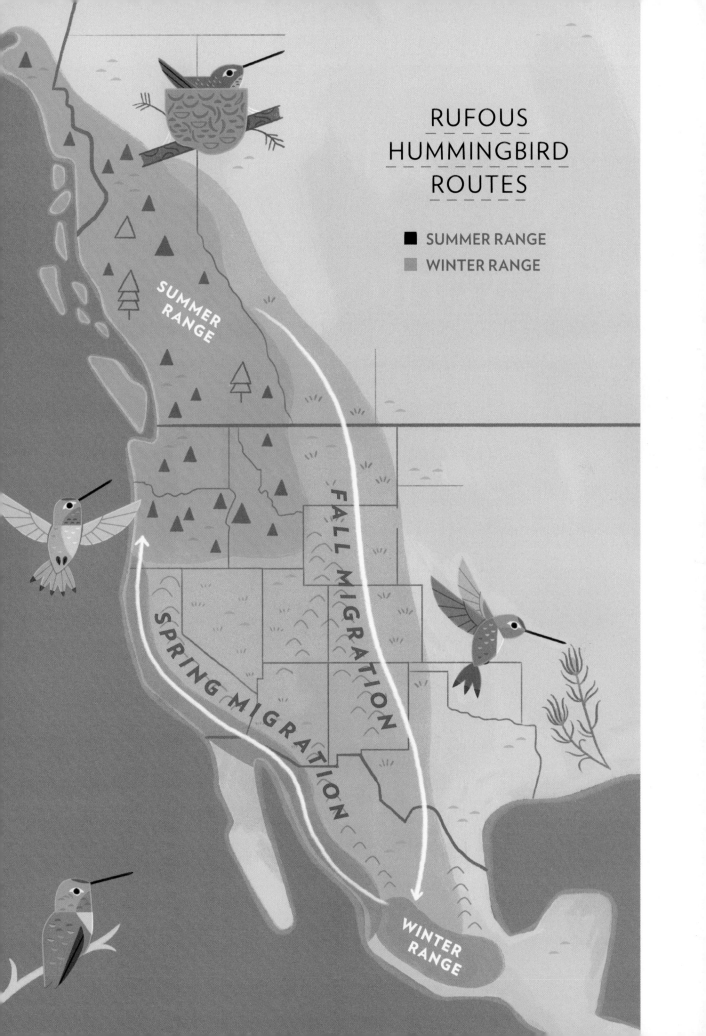

RUFOUS
HUMMINGBIRD
ROUTES

■ SUMMER RANGE
■ WINTER RANGE

SUMMER RANGE

FALL MIGRATION

SPRING MIGRATION

WINTER RANGE

Perennial Nectar Favorites

Attract more hummingbirds year after year with flowers that require less time, maintenance and money

Ruby-throated hummingbird at John Clayton trumpet honeysuckle

Cardinal flower stems offer many blooms for ruby-throated hummingbirds.

NOTHING IS SWEETER than seeing a hummingbird visit your yard. Sugar-water feeders are one way to attract these vibrant birds, but an even better bet is an abundance of flowering plants that they love. Grow perennials to keep hummers coming back each year.

Plant with Purpose

"If we want to truly support birds, our first instinct must be to create native habitat," says Becca Rodomsky-Bish, a project leader for the Cornell Lab of Ornithology. "While sugar-water feeders are a fun way to pull birds in close to our homes, they don't resolve the long-term issue that many birds, such as hummingbirds, can have, which is where to forage for native food resources."

Hummingbirds may consume about half their body weight in nectar each day, feeding approximately every 10 to 15 minutes. (They also eat small insects, especially during the nesting season.) All that sipping means that they require access to many blooms every day. Native perennials are a terrific option to fill that demand.

"Plants that are attuned to your region will bloom and produce what is needed, when it is needed," Becca says. "Provide a variety of plants that produce flowers at different times in the season to best align with the resources that hummingbirds require to successfully recover after long migrations, raise their young and fuel up to prepare for their fall migrations."

Most North American hummers migrate farther south for winter. They make long journeys in spring and fall and need ample food along the way. Native perennials' bloom cycles ensure that your garden is stocked with nectar throughout the seasons.

Bee balm is native to North America and attracts pollinators such as the ruby-throated hummingbird.

Find the Perfect Match

In most regions, perennials go dormant for the colder months and their shoots grow anew in spring. In warmer zones, perennials are often evergreen, though they may only bloom in certain months. Either way, perennials tend to require a little less maintenance and cost than replanting annuals each year.

Since perennials are going to be with you for the long haul, be sure to choose them carefully. Do some research before buying. A potted plant that looks pretty at the nursery could turn into a monster that spreads underground or crowds out everything nearby.

Look at tags to find out how tall and wide a plant will get. Also, talk to a nursery specialist about whether the perennial is fast-growing, which might mean it requires more pruning or dividing each year. As with any shrub, tree or flower, review the requirements for sun, water and soil type. Choose some flowering plants, such as bleeding hearts or columbines, specifically for shady spots in your yard. If you really love a plant

The pretty, yet muted blooms of penstemon attract hummingbirds and look perfect in a monochromatic garden.

Salvia's long flowers are perfectly shaped for ruby-throated hummingbirds.

As its name suggests, butterfly weed is beloved by both beneficial insects and birds.

but are worried about the conditions it needs, try growing it in a container instead of straight in the ground. This allows you to control the soil type and amount of sun the plant receives.

For perennials that attract hummers, one type tends to be better than all the rest. "Hummingbirds prefer plants that produce tubular-shaped flowers, as they generally contain the most nectar," says Becca. And while the old wisdom about plants with red flowers holds true, she promises that hummingbirds will visit blossoms of any hue, as long as they provide plenty of nectar.

Little Effort, Big Reward

Generally lower maintenance than annuals, perennials do require a little care after they're planted and once established. Some types,

especially those that grow from rhizomes or bulbs, should be divided every few years. Dig them up, roots and all, then use a sharp spade to split them apart into smaller sections. Spread them out and replant.

Perennial shrubs may need pruning each year, but be sure to research the right time for this chore. Many spring flowering shrubs set buds early in summer, so if you prune late in the growing season, you could end up with no blooms the following year.

Adding perennials for hummingbirds is an easy way to benefit both birds and humans. We get the joy of seeing these colorful jewels up close. And hummingbirds find a more robust environment that provides food and shelter. As Becca says, "Adding native perennials pays it forward for generations of wildlife."

A black-chinned hummingbird sips nectar from a columbine bloom.

TOP PERENNIALS

Nectar-producing plants that return every year.

- Beardtongue, Zones 4 to 9
- Bee balm, Zones 3 to 8
- Butterfly weed, Zones 3 to 9
- Cardinal flower, Zones 3 to 9
- Chuparosa, Zones 8 to 11
- Columbine, Zones 3 to 9
- Goldenrod, Zones 3 to 9
- Native honeysuckle, Zones 3 to 10
- Phlox, Zones 3 to 9
- Salvia, Zones 3 to 11

Hummingbird Magnets

Attract these busy fliers with nectar-packed salvias

Rufous hummingbird

1

MADE FOR EACH OTHER
A hummingbird's long tongue, which can extend to about twice the length of its bill, is perfectly adapted to salvia's long tubular flowers.

1. Hummingbird Falls Bodacious salvia

SALVIA X GUARANITICA, ZONES 7 TO 8 OR ANNUAL

Bodacious is one of the first salvias for hanging baskets. Its draping quality makes it a perfect spiller or ground cover. It reaches 2 feet tall while spreading up to 3 feet wide. The blossoms appear in spring and bloom continuously through fall in full sun to part shade. Use as an annual in cool climates.

Why we love it: You'll easily spot visiting hummingbirds when this salvia is hung at eye level.

2. Rose Rhapsody Ballet meadow sage

SALVIA PRATENSIS, ZONES 3 TO 9

The soft pink blooms have a hooded appearance and make wonderful cut flowers. Rose Rhapsody welcomes deadheading in spring and can be easily divided to plant elsewhere in the garden. Grow in a spot with consistent moisture for best results. It has an upright form and attracts hummingbirds and bees, while also being deer resistant.

Why we love it: The plant tolerates heat and humidity as well as a range of soils.

3. Heatwave Breeze salvia

SALVIA MICROPHYLLA X GREGGII, ZONES 6 TO 10 OR ANNUAL

This cultivar has an upright and rounded habit that reaches a height and width of 2 to 3 feet. The rich purple blooms welcome hummingbirds with their large tubular shape. After the first flush of blooms, trim the plant back to encourage even more flowers.

Why we love it: Developed as a water-wise plant, Breeze needs well-draining soil and tolerates drought.

4. Cold Hardy Pink bush sage

SALVIA GREGGII, ZONES 6 TO 10

Bred from a Texas native, Cold Hardy Pink sage is ideal in a border or container. The rosy pink bloomer invites all sorts of pollinators. It grows in most of the United States, but thrives in the Southwest.

Why we love it: Small-space gardeners will appreciate its compact size—the plant tops out at around 20 inches.

5. Strata mealycup sage

SALVIA FARINACEA, ZONES 8 TO 11

Bicolor blue and white flowers lend additional interest to this award-winning mealycup sage. It stands at 2 feet tall and tolerates heavy rain, heat or drought. The green foliage and blue petals add gorgeous cool tones to summer gardens.

Why we love it:
In a sunny border, Strata blooms continuously and is mostly pest-free. Cut flowers can be easily dried for arrangements.

6. Rockin' Golden Delicious golden leaved pineapple sage

SALVIA ELEGANS, ZONES 8 TO 11 OR ANNUAL

For most gardeners, this salvia stands out for its vibrant yellow-green foliage. In areas with a long growing season, the plant also produces fire-engine red flowers in fall, attracting butterflies and hummers.

Why we love it: Pineapple sage's blooms are lusciously fragrant—and edible. Use them in salads and garnishes.

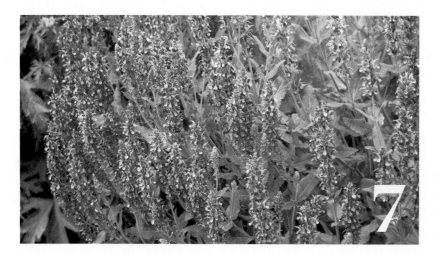

7. Blue Hill meadow sage

SALVIA X SYLVESTRIS, ZONES 4 TO 8

Blue Hill is a compact salvia that's best planted in containers, at the edge of a border or as a taller ground cover in full sun. It's salt tolerant, so try planting it along driveways or sidewalks. It prefers drier soil in winter and moist to moderately moist soils in the summer.

Why we love it: It produces beautiful cut flowers, and it resists pests such as deer and rabbits, too.

Bees, such as this bumblebee at a pitcher sage, love salvias just as much as hummingbirds do.

8. Lady in Red dwarf scarlet salvia

SALVIA COCCINEA, ZONES 8 TO 10 OR ANNUAL

Chosen for its high performance, dwarf size and early flowers, this plant is an All-America Selections winner. It grows 12 to 14 inches tall, with brilliant red blooms from May into November—it can even handle a light frost.

Why we love it: The warm colors are like beacons to hummingbirds on the move or during migration.

9. Pitcher sage

SALVIA AZUREA VAR. GRANDIFLORA, ZONES 5 TO 9

This perennial is cold hardy up to Zone 5 and comes in a range of blue hues as well as white. It looks great planted by tall grasses in a meadow or as a shrubby border. Cut back the plant's fragrant stems in late spring to keep it more compact and to promote new blooms.

Why we love it: A giant in the salvia world, it can reach 3 to 5 feet in height and grows nearly as wide.

OTHER FAVORITES

- Cardinal flower (Lobelia cardinalis)
- Coral honeysuckle (Lonicera sempervirens)
- Great blue lobelia (Lobelia siphilitica)
- Scarlet bee balm (Monarda didyma)
- Trumpet vine (Campsis radicans)

10. Lyreleaf sage

SALVIA LYRATA, ZONES 5 TO 8

This sage stands between 1 and 2 feet tall. In the winter, a purple-green rosette of leaves marks its place in the garden. It blooms in full sun from April through June with white, blue or violet flowers. It's ideal in rain gardens and tolerates some flooding.

Why we love it: Use it as a ground cover after it blooms—you can even mow the plants for a tidier look.

Male Calliopes puff out a flashy group of neck feathers, also known as the gorget, to woo potential mates.

Small and Fiesty Fliers

Meet Calliope hummingbirds and attract them with native plants

Female Calliope at El Paso skyrocket flowers

MEASURING A MERE 3 inches long and weighing roughly the same as a pingpong ball, the Calliope hummingbird is incredibly tiny. In fact, Eric Rasmussen, avian scientist at the MPG Ranch in Montana's Bitterroot Valley, points out that this hummingbird is the smallest bird seen in North America.

Pops of Purple

Look for several key clues to identify this diminutive species. Both males and females sport glossy, bright green plumage on their heads and backs, with white on their underparts. Males have stripes of magenta along the throat, while females and juveniles have a bit of cinnamon color underneath. Look closely, too, at a Calliope's tail and wings. "When they are perched, their wingtips tend to protrude just below the tail tip," Eric says.

Take Flight

Calliopes focus on flowers as they travel north for up to 2,800 miles mainly through the interior West in early spring. As the wildflower meadows of the Rocky Mountains bloom, Calliopes fly uphill, where they mate and raise their young before following the mountains as they travel back south in fall.

"Males arrive early and stake out nectar resources," Eric says. To impress females, males fly high into the air, then dive down while making a buzzing noise with their tail feathers. A male will also hover in front of a female with his dazzling neck feathers ruffled forward while making a sound similar to a bumblebee.

The location of the 1½-inch-wide nests can vary, but they're typically several feet up in a conifer tree. The female alone cares for the young until they are ready for the first flight around three weeks old.

Attract Calliopes

At every age, hummingbirds need a constant food supply to maintain their energy.

"I strongly encourage planting native flowers," says Eric. "That is the best way to help hummingbirds." Choose native options that bloom early in the season and continue through the fall.

If you put out sugar-water feeders to attract Calliopes or other hummers, you shouldn't use red dye in the mixture.

Eric notes that hummingbirds prefer shallow water features that gently bubble. "They need a little place to perch," he adds.

Enjoy a front-row seat to Calliope hummingbird visits by creating an oasis in your own backyard for these tiny fliers.

NO-FEAR FLIERS
During breeding season, male Calliopes are brave enough to chase off much larger birds, even hawks, from their territory.

INSECT SNACK TIME
Besides feeding on nectar, Calliope hummingbirds perch on branches before diving to snatch and eat insects from midair.

BEST BLOOMS
Choose native plants with smaller blossoms to accommodate Calliope hummingbirds.
Anise hyssop
Beardtongue
Bee balm
Coral bells
Golden currant

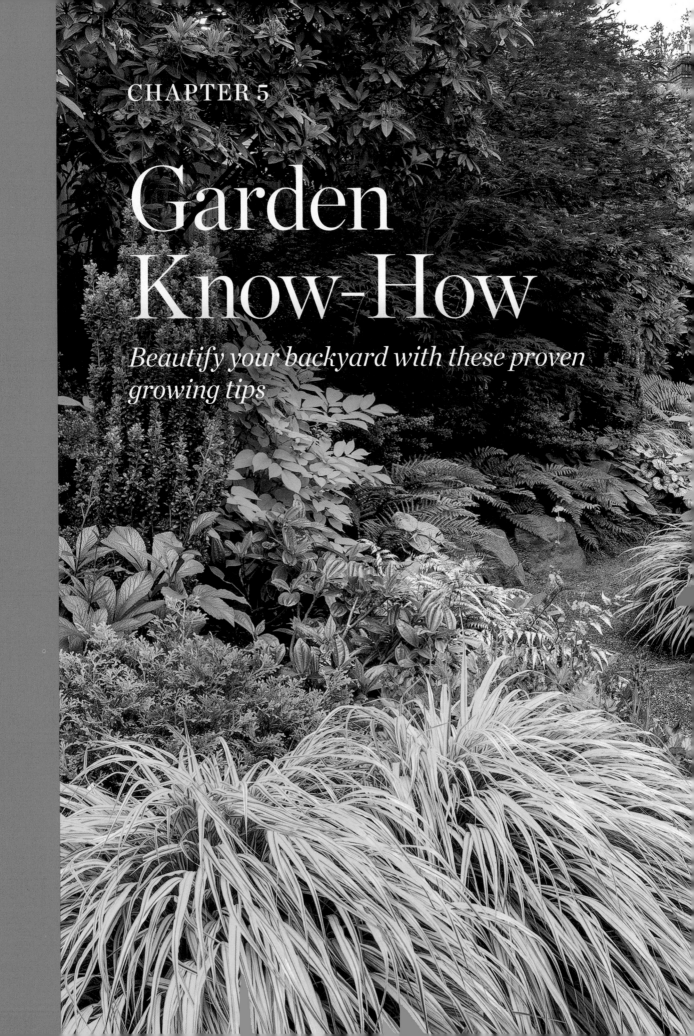

CHAPTER 5

Garden Know-How

Beautify your backyard with these proven growing tips

I was pleasantly surprised to find this Pacific tree frog hanging out in my backyard daylily garden during the summer. This type of frog is frequently spotted in Washington state. I took this photo with my Pentax DSLR camera.

Tami Shaughnessy
OLYMPIA, WASHINGTON

Bloom Tales

Find inspiration for your springtime garden plans among these gorgeous flower photos

Beautiful shades of blue and gray adorn this dainty blue copper butterfly perched on some goldenrod in the foothills of Boise, Idaho. I shot this photo with a Canon PowerShot SX60 HS camera.

Gretchen Fitzgerald-Teel
BOISE, IDAHO

► My first time ever planting zinnias from seed resulted in this beautiful bloom. I noticed the interesting folds on the petals, as well as the structure, aesthetic and color mixture in the center. It was a delight to capture a perfectly bold zinnia.

Nancy Rau
NEW BRIGHTON, PENNSYLVANIA

▼ Bumblebees were busy at work on these dahlia flowers, making the photo even more beautiful. I took this in summer with a Canon EOS 7D Mark II and a Canon EF 400 mm super telephoto lens.

Richard A. Schultz
WAUSAU, WISCONSIN

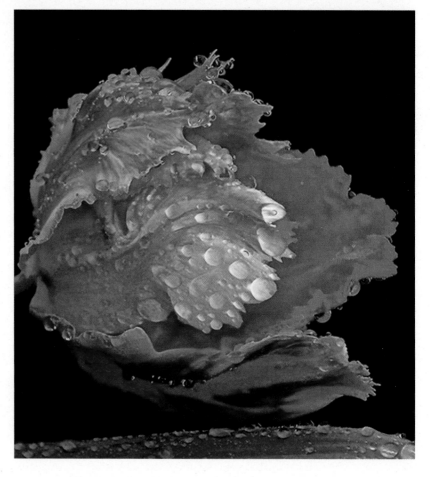

▲ **While on an evening** stroll at the Sarah P. Duke Gardens on the Duke University campus, I captured this beautiful view of a waterlily with a dragonfly on it as the sun set.

Vianne Pendleton
RALEIGH, NORTH CAROLINA

▶ **As a longtime** gardener from the Northeast, I was concerned that I wouldn't be able to have my beautiful spring garden when I moved to Arizona. While the spring weather is milder here than in the Northeast, it proved to have the temperatures that bulbs need. I filled my garden with various types of tulips. I've always loved parrot tulips in particular, and on one early morning, after a soft, light rain, this one looked too dreamy.

Diane Hendler
CORNVILLE, ARIZONA

I have one poppy in my backyard—it's one of the first flowers to bloom in my garden. It looked so good after a rain that I grabbed my camera. When the poppy bloom dies off, I know spring is over and summer is here.

Dean Tyler
HANCOCK, MAINE

Easy Breezy Gardening

Seven tips for a beautiful low-maintenance yard with minimal fuss and effort

A gravel pathway with stepping stones is an easy, water-saving solution.

1. Water Less Frequently

Choose drought tolerant plants, trees and shrubs that require less water to thrive. It makes sense to reduce the number of times you need to lug a full watering can or hose around the yard, plus watering restrictions are a reality in many areas. Plenty of beautiful native options work in a variety of climates and soils with little water.

The keys are to carefully match the plant to its new growing conditions and to water it consistently until it's established. Once it has a good root system, it will grow with minimal supplemental water.

2. Let Go of Lawn Care

Many folks love their grass lawns but, frankly, an attractive lawn can require lots of upkeep. Replace a patch of grass with an appropriate ground cover plant to slash your chore time without sacrificing a lush, lovely yard.

Swap turf with a ground cover that grows in problem spots such as shady, hot or rocky areas. Check with your local university extension service for a list of plants suited for your area.

3. Pick Healthy Options

Many new trees and shrubs are bred to resist disease and pests. They tend to be healthier and more self-sufficient and need fewer treatments. Plus, they're more likely to last, which decreases the odds that you'll need to dig one up and replace it in the future.

4. Go Small

Plant breeders are also developing smaller plants. This means garden favorites can fit into small spaces without extensive pruning. Dwarf

Enjoy an easy-to-maintain patio dotted with low-maintenance plants.

Globe blue spruce, upright Skyrocket juniper, and smaller ninebarks, such as Summer Wine or Little Devil, all have fantastic qualities and require minimal pruning to fit into tinier spaces.

5. Add Living Space

Patio pavers set in a grid and surrounded by landscaping rocks make an elegant, simple and environmentally friendly surface for an outdoor lounge set. Walkways, patios, courtyards and other elements add a bit of magic to any yard while also reducing landscaping chores.

Choose materials and designs that allow rain to permeate the soil, irrigate surrounding plantings, minimize erosion and prevent runoff. These include organic mulches, gravel, crushed stone and permeable pavers.

6. Make Room for Mulch

Weed less by mulching. Apply a layer of wood chips or bark at least a few inches thick every two or three years. That way the soil will also retain moisture more readily, meaning you can water less.

Avoid turning the soil, which

exposes dormant weed seeds to moisture and air and may cause them to sprout. Instead, let the earthworms from your compost or healthy soil do the cultivating for you.

7. Skip Fussy Flowers

Gardeners love roses, but most need a bounty of water, fertilizer and attention to look their best. You shouldn't give up everything you love, but choose your plantings carefully. If the majority of your landscape is relatively carefree, you'll have more time to keep your finicky plants happy.

Early-Blooming Shrubs

Greet spring with pretty plants that shine all season

FABULOUS FRUITS
After its floral show, dwarf Russian almond produces nuts that are about ¾ inch long and have a hard, hairy shell.

1

1. Dwarf Russian almond

PRUNUS TENELLA, ZONES 2 TO 6

This modest-sized shrub bookends the growing season with showy rose red spring flowers and yellow-orange fall color. It prefers full sun, tolerates a range of soil types and is fairly drought resistant. Ruth's 100 produces abundant blooms on a compact plant.

Why we love it: Flowers appear early and attract butterflies. Plus, the plant provides food and cover for backyard birds and wildlife.

2. Paperbush plant

EDGEWORTHIA CHRYSANTHA., ZONES 7 TO 9

Leafless stems provide interest in winter, while creamy yellow flowers with a spicy scent attract pollinators such as bees and butterflies in late winter or early spring. The Gold Finch variety tolerates humidity and heat, and Grandiflora boasts larger flowers.

Why we love it: Dark green leaves turn rich yellow in fall, adding to its year-round appeal. And its bark can be used to make paper, hence its common name.

3. Bush cherry

PRUNUS JACQUEMANTII., ZONES 5 TO 8

Here's a cherry that southern gardeners can also enjoy. Rose-colored buds open to fragrant pink flowers that attract butterflies and other pollinators. The green leaves are a larval host for the eastern tiger swallowtail butterfly and turn yellow in the fall. Grow in full sun with moist, well-draining soil.

Why we love it: The fruit, which ranges from red to plum purple, attracts birds to the landscape.

4. Cornelian cherry dogwood

CORNUS MAS., ZONES 4 TO 8

Welcome spring with bright yellow flowers that appear earlier than forsythia's blooms. It prefers full sun or part shade, and rich, moist, well-draining soil. Leaves turn purplish red in fall, and flaky bark adds winter interest.

Why we love it: The red fruits are edible, but they are tastier made into preserves, jellies and pies. Or leave them for the birds to enjoy.

5. Dwarf fothergilla

FOTHERGILLA GARDENII, ZONES 4 TO 9

The fothergilla is a slow grower that sends up additional shoots, forming a colony. Remove any unwanted stems to control its size. The blue-green leaves turn vibrant red, orange and yellow in the fall. Grow it in full sun to part shade, and in rich, moist, acidic soil.

Why we love it: White, honey-scented bottlebrush flowers attract bees and other beneficial pollinators.

6. Pearlbush

EXOCHORDA RACEMOSA, ZONES 4 TO 8

Place this large shrub where you are sure to enjoy the spring floral display. In midspring Pearl-like flower buds open into white flowers, followed by interesting seed capsules. Use it as a hedge or include it in a mixed or shrub border. Prune the shrub immediately after it blooms for best results.

Why we love it: Growing in full sun to part shade, this shrub is low maintenance as well as heat and drought tolerant.

7. Daphne

DAPHNE, ZONES 4 TO 8

Choose from a variety of sizes and spring bloom times. Grow in full sun to part shade where the lovely fragrant flowers can be enjoyed. Daphnes prefer moist, well-draining soil and protection from winter wind and sun.

Why we love it: The evergreen leaves of some cultivars and the variegated leaves of Carol Mackie make daphnes a welcome addition to a home garden of any size.

8. Flowering quince

CHAENOMELES SPECIOSA, ZONES 4 TO 9

Quince's white, pink or red flowers are followed by an apple-like fruit that turns yellow in the fall (make it into preserves and jellies). Leaves emerge a bronzy red before turning green in summer. Grow in full sun for the best flowering.
Why we love it: The colorful flowers attract butterflies and hummingbirds.

9. Vernal witch hazel

HAMAMELIS VERNALIS, ZONES 4 TO 8

Enjoy seasons of color from this North American native. Fragrant flowers are golden yellow, orange or burgundy-red. Leaves emerge reddish bronze, turn green in the summer and shift to yellow in fall. The best flowering happens in full sun, but the plant tolerates part shade.
Why we love it: This beauty attracts songbirds, but deer leave it alone.

MORE SPRING STUNNERS

- Azalea
- Bridalwreath spirea
- Camellia
- Forsythia
- Rhododendron
- Sweet box
- Viburnum
- Wintersweet

10. Japanese pieris

PIERIS JAPONICA, ZONES 4 TO 7

Grow as a large shrub or small tree in full sun to part shade. It prefers moist, well-draining, acidic soil, as well as a location where its evergreen leaves are protected from winter winds.
Why we love it: The showy buds that form in late summer add beauty to the winter garden before opening into white flowers in early spring.

Made for Shade

Low-light spaces call for bright-idea plants with perks

SHADE GARDENS offer many advantages. Birds and pollinators need them for food, nesting and shelter. Even gardeners benefit from cooler shaded areas. But finding plants that bring color, interest and activity to your shady spaces isn't always easy.

To liven up low-light areas, consider plants known for bold foliage. Invite different leaf colors and textures to mingle, such as frilly fern fronds and the lily pad–like leaves of ligularia plants. And many colorful bloomers thrive in partial shade. Cool or light colors such as whites, pinks and blues pop in even the darkest corners of the garden.

Finally, bring a buzz of pollinator activity. Plants native to your region should be your first choice. Here are some plant picks to get you started.

A lush shade garden full of hostas, coral bells, ferns and Japanese forest grass

Fanciful Foliage

Leaves bring as much beauty to a shade garden as blooms. Available in an array of sizes, shapes and colors, plants with unique foliage add visual interest and diversity. Grow them in multiples for big impact.

1. JAPANESE PAINTED FERN

ANISOCAMPIUM NIPONICUM,
ZONES 2 TO 9

For sophisticated texture and color, consider this woodland favorite. One of the showiest cultivars is Pictum, with silvery gray fronds and burgundy red stems. For a touch of flair, try Crested Surf, which sports two frilly tips on every frond.

2. LUNGWORT

PULMONARIA, ZONES 3 TO 8

This low-growing beauty boasts fuzzy spotted or striped leaves that rest below spring blooms in hues of blue, purple, pink, red or white. Morning sun and afternoon shade keep them looking fresh.

3. BARRENWORT

EPIMEDIUM, ZONES 4 TO 8

Dainty flowers in pink, purple, yellow or white appear in spring, but this plant's main draw is its durable heart-shaped leaves. They make a trouble-free ground cover, tolerating both dry and moist shade.

4. SUN KING JAPANESE SPIKENARD

ARALIA CORDATA, ZONES 3 TO 9

With large chartreuse leaves that thrive in partial shade, this plant reaches 3 to 6 feet tall and wide. A deer-resistant stunner that lives up to its regal name, it was the Perennial Plant Association's 2020 Plant of the Year.

Colorful Characters

Some plants flower well in shade, especially when given morning sun. These specimens' showy blooms set the shade garden ablaze in color. But they have a lot more going for them, too—attractive foliage, interesting forms and more.

5. CORAL BELLS

HEUCHERA, ZONES 3 TO 9

Available in a wide range of leaf colors, such as amber, bronze, green, gold, pink and purple, these powerhouse plants are shade garden all-stars. Plus, the tiny flowers held aloft on wiry stems make good cut flowers.

6. BEE BALM

MONARDA, ZONES 3 TO 8

This classic beauty produces more flowers in sun but can flourish when in shade, especially in hot climates. Most regions have a native or hardy species with pink, purple or red blooms that catch the eye with their spiky form.

7. BELLFLOWER

CAMPANULA, ZONES 3 TO 9

This huge plant family offers blooms in many shapes and sizes, though most come in hues of pink, blue and violet. A perfect option for partial shade is Serbian bellflower, a low-growing ground cover with starry bluish purple flowers.

8. BRUNNERA

BRUNNERA MACROPHYLLA, ZONES 3 TO 8

Its heart-shaped leaves with a silvery sheen and contrasting veins are unpalatable to deer.

9

Sporting blue or white flowers in spring, the foliage of newer cultivars such as Silver Heart, Sea Heart or Jack Frost shine throughout the growing season.

Hummingbird Happiness

Many hummingbird-preferred flowers grow best in sun, but some do offer blooms bearing rich nectar in shade. Bees, butterflies and other pollinators will also find and appreciate them.

9. COLUMBINE

AQUILEGIA, ZONES 3 TO 9

Native species bloom in an array of colors, including red, yellow, orange, blue and purple. The bell-shaped flowers are nectar powerhouses. These 2- to 3-foot-tall perennials self-sow and prefer soil that drains quickly.

10. INDIAN PINK

SPIGELIA MARILANDICA, ZONES 5 TO 9

This 1-to-2-foot-tall native deserves a place in more shade gardens. The drought tolerant, clump-forming plants produce trumpet-shaped red and yellow flowers that hummers flock to. Extend the bloom time by deadheading.

11. LIGULARIA

LIGULARIA DENTATA, ZONES 4 TO 9

These perennials boast an assortment of leaf shapes and sizes. If it's butterflies you're after, try Britt Marie Crawford with golden, daisylike flowers or Bottle Rocket with gold spires of blooms. Plant in moist soil.

10

11

12. HOSTA

HOSTA, ZONES 3 TO 9

Mainly grown for its impressive foliage, this shade-garden favorite has flowers in hues from white to lavender that attract nectar lovers. To create a hummingbird buffet, plant fragrant varieties near red-blooming plants.

Best for Butterflies

Butterflies float toward many of the same plants beloved by other insects and hummingbirds, but they especially appreciate a shady landing pad where they can comfortably sip nectar.

13. CARDINAL FLOWER

LOBELIA CARDINALIS, ZONES 3 TO 9

With bright red or pink tubular blooms, this native does well in sun or part shade, provided it gets plenty of water. After its vibrant flowers fade, enjoy the fresh foliage and possibly a second bloom if you cut back the old spikes.

14. GERANIUM

GERANIUM, ZONES 3 TO 8

Native geraniums fit a wide range of growing conditions. Blossoms in shades of pink, blue or purple grow on mounded foliage and are easy for butterflies to find and enjoy.

15. WHITE WOOD ASTER

EURYBIA DIVARICATA, ZONES 3 TO 8

Drought tolerant and easy to grow, this native blooms late in the season, providing butterflies with last-minute energy. Tolerant of heavy shade, it grows 1 to 2 feet tall with a plethora of flowers.

16. TURTLEHEAD

CHELONE LYONII, ZONES 3 TO 8

Named for its flowers' resemblance to open-mouthed turtles, this late-summer bloomer attracts winged visitors with its pink, purple or white blooms. A perfect pick for rain gardens, it's also deer resistant.

Perks of Propagating

A step-by-step guide to multiplying your most prized succulents

Propagating leaf cuttings

1. Gather supplies

When it comes to tools, the most important thing is to sterilize them. "Make sure you're not using dirty tools, because it's very easy to pass bacteria or viral infection from one plant to another," Aaron says. Whether you use a bonsai knife, Japanese snips or clippers, clean your tools and wipe them with isopropyl alcohol before cutting. You'll also need clean pots, open flats or liner trays with drainage holes, and succulent potting soil.

2. Make the cut

You can root a stem of any size from a multi-branching succulent, Aaron says. Make a cut right below a growth node and strip off extra leaves, leaving two or three at the top. "You need some leaves for the plant to feed itself, but unnecessary leaves might take energy away from the rooting process," he says. Stick the cut end 1 to 2 inches into a porous, fast-draining soil mix that can dry quickly. "You never want to have wet feet with succulents; they will rot," he adds. Compress the soil so the cutting stands upright.

3. Peel a leaf

A few leaves can produce many succulent rosettes, Aaron says. Select thick, healthy leaves near the base. Detach them carefully and completely by grasping each leaf where it meets the stem and peeling it downward.

"If you just rip it off, you'll lose all the marrow stem tissue and the leaf will rot away," he says.

Set the detached leaves flat on the surface of a damp bed of 75% perlite and 25% ground-up fir bark, redwood bark or peat. Sometimes you'll get two or three rosettes from one leaf.

Propagating is a free and easy way to get even more beautiful succulents.

4. Find the right location

Cuttings root better in bright, airy and humid spots away from direct sunlight or heat. Rooting time depends on the species but might begin after two weeks. After about four weeks, pull gently on your cutting to see if it has rooted. You will have a fully rooted cutting to transplant into a 4-inch pot or a 1-gallon container within five weeks, Aaron says.

5. Water just the right amount

Cuttings need regular moisture until they grow roots, but be sure you are not overwatering. "The key is to water infrequently but deeply," Aaron says. "Let the soil approach dryness between watering."

Once fully rooted, succulents store water in their roots, stems and leaves, making them drought tolerant plants.

6. Watch for pests

Take cuttings from your healthy plants only. Good airflow helps prevent infestations of mealybugs and gnats, Aaron says.

"Mealybugs are really detrimental to succulents, causing deformation of the leaves. And with young plants, you have to be especially vigilant about keeping them away," Aaron says.

7. Have fun experimenting

"Propagating is like mad science; it's so fun," Aaron says. "Once you get good at propagating from succulent cuttings, try your hand at woody perennials and softwood and hardwood cuttings. Succulents are a great way to learn."

Patented plants should not be propagated; it may be illegal to create new cuttings. Patent fees support breeders and their work to create new plants.

11 BEST SUCCULENTS FOR PROPAGATING

- Ghost echeveria
- Lola echeveria
- Perle von Nurnberg echeveria
- Fred Ives graptoveria
- Ghost plant
- California Sunset graptosedum
- Mother of thousands
- Burro's tail
- Jelly bean plant
- Hens-and-chicks
- String of pearls

Whimsical Perennials

Add easy-care flowers to create a cottage garden style

1

1. Violet Profusion salvia

SALVIA NEMOROSA, ZONES 3 TO 8
Add a bold pop of purple with this fragrant and wildlife-friendly salvia. This compact perennial tops out at 16 inches tall and 20 inches wide and makes an eye-catching edge along a pathway, fence or garden bed.
Why we love it: As a reblooming salvia, it can produce a second burst of purple flowers in early autumn. Shear back the plants after the first floral fade to encourage a quick turnaround.

2. Moonbeam threadleaf coreopsis

COREOPSIS VERTICILLATA, ZONES 3 TO 9
Also called tickseed, this compact plant sold by Monrovia has lacy foliage and grows up to 18 inches tall and 24 inches wide. By early summer the plants are smothered in lemon yellow daisylike flowers that persist for months. For constant blooms, gently shear it after its first flowers fade.
Why we love it: It's an award-winning perennial that is long lived and easy to grow.

3. Cat's Meow catmint

NEPETA FAASSENII, ZONES 3 TO 8
A perfect perennial for a flower border, this colorful bloomer grows up to 20 inches tall and 36 inches wide. Unlike most catmint types, which tend to flop, this selection has tidy, upright growth. Its purple flower spikes last from early summer through autumn, attracting bees, butterflies and hummingbirds.
Why we love it: Catmint is drought tolerant and resistant to grazing from deer and rabbits.

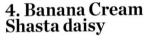

4. Banana Cream Shasta daisy

LEUCANTHEMUM SUPERBUM, ZONES 5 TO 9
This daisy has massive yellow blooms that mature to a creamy white, resulting in a multicolored display in spring and summer. Up to 18 inches tall and 24 inches wide, it makes a great border or container plant.
Why we love it: One of the biggest benefits of planting a cottage garden is cutting flowers for bouquets. These Shasta daisy blooms last at least two weeks in a vase.

5. Blue Fortune anise hyssop

AGASTACHE, ZONES 4 TO 9

This multipurpose perennial checks all the boxes—it's pest resistant and drought tolerant, and it flowers for months, producing clouds of pale lavender blooms. Pair it with rudbeckia or purple coneflower for an impressive late-summer display.

Why we love it: Its leaves and flowers have the fragrance and flavor of black licorice. Steep them for an aromatic cup of tea, or add them to salads and smoothies.

6. Gay Butterflies butterfly weed

ASCLEPIAS TUBEROSA, ZONES 4 TO 11

Welcome butterflies and bees to your cottage garden with several clumps of this low-care perennial that's both drought tolerant and pest resistant. Sold by Monrovia, this plant showcases blooms from mid-to-late summer with fiery gold, yellow and scarlet flower clusters.

Why we love it: Butterfly weed is a species of milkweed, which is the only type of host plant for monarch butterflies.

7. Perfectly Picasso speedwell

VERONICA LONGIFOLIA, ZONES 4 TO 9

Paint the garden pretty with the bubblegum pink flowers of this pollinator-friendly perennial that grows 2 feet tall and wide. Its graceful, dense flower spikes put on a show for up to six weeks beginning in midsummer.

Why we love it: The slender flower spikes bloom from the bottom up, creating a striking two-toned appearance.

8. Raspberry Wine bee balm

MONARDA DIDYMA, ZONES 4 TO 9

Bee balm is a classic beloved by cottage gardeners, as well as hummingbirds and bees. This bold cultivar with aromatic foliage boasts masses of raspberry red blossoms. With plants that grow 2 to 3 feet tall and wide, it's perfect for both large and small gardens.

Why we love it: It's a low-maintenance perennial that's resistant to deer and powdery mildew.

9. David garden phlox

PHLOX PANICULATA, ZONES 4 TO 8

Reliable, long flowering and disease resistant, this phlox is an outstanding choice. Plants grow up to 4 feet tall, with strong stems topped with large clusters of fragrant white blooms. Unlike other cultivars, David offers excellent resistance to powdery mildew.

Why we love it: This summer staple is extremely vigorous, and its nectar-rich flowers entice hummingbirds and butterflies to the garden.

ROWS OF ROSES

Plant long-lasting color with these cottage classics.

Look for heirloom or rugosa roses that are hardy and fragrant. Try the Blanc Double de Coubert or a selection of repeat-blooming David Austin roses.

10. Tangerine Dream coneflower

ECHINACEA, ZONES 4 TO 9

This sun-loving coneflower with a honey scent lights up the summer garden with large bright orange flowers. The compact beauty grows up to 2 feet tall and wide.

Why we love it: Coneflowers are pollinator magnets. Once the flowers fade, the seed heads feed birds such as goldfinches and blue jays.

Taking On Invasives

Tips for identifying, removing and replacing problematic plants

Certain invasives, such as this purple loosestrife, look beautiful but can create big garden problems.

THE TAG AT THE GARDEN CENTER MAY SAY that a plant is "long blooming, low maintenance and fast growing." If this description seems too good to be true, it's because it sometimes is. Many plants once recommended for the garden have since left our carefully curated landscapes and invaded nearby natural areas. Once invasive plants gain a foothold in natural spaces, they crowd out the native plants that birds, pollinators and other wildlife depend upon.

Invasives are defined as nonnative, adaptable plants that reproduce by seeds, stems and roots, which are either spread by wind, deposited by birds, or carried into new areas by people, pets and visiting wildlife.

Buy Suitable Plants

To avoid accidentally adding troublesome plants to your yard, do a bit of research before purchasing. Check with your local nature center, the Department of Natural Resources or a nearby university extension service for lists of known invasive species in your region. In addition, the U.S. Forest Service (fs.usda.gov) and Invasive Plant Atlas of the United States (invasiveplantatlas.org) are helpful online resources.

Pay Attention to Decor

Door swags and wreaths can also contribute to this problem. These decorations can contain invasive plants, such as teasel and oriental bittersweet. Their seeds are released from the arrangements into nearby gardens, eventually making their way to natural spaces.

Get Rid of Tick Havens

Removing invasive plants also can help reduce disease-carrying tick

Kudzu

Honeysuckle

populations. Studies have found that the presence of Japanese barberry and honeysuckle bushes create the perfect habitat for both deer and the ticks that feed on them.

Weed Them Out

Remove and discard small invasive plants, including the roots, as recommended by your local municipality. Many allow you to place these in the trash since they will be buried in a landfill. Avoid composting invasive plants unless your pile is hot enough (150 to 180 degrees) to kill the plants, roots and seeds.

You will need to use different techniques for larger tree and shrub specimens. You can slowly kill problem trees by either removing a 6-inch strip of bark around the base of the plant or painting the bottom 12 inches of the trunk with a recommended herbicide. You can also choose to cut the plant to the ground, then treat the stump with either a brush or total vegetation killer to prevent the stump and roots from sprouting. As always, carefully read and follow label directions.

Add Natives Instead

Have fun replacing troublemaking plants with better alternatives. Select native plants suited to your yard's growing conditions and available space and, of course, look for options that support birds and pollinators.

MOST COMMON INVASIVES

- Barberries
- Buckthorn
- Chinese and Japanese wisterias
- English ivy
- Garlic mustard
- Japanese honeysuckle
- Japanese knotweed
- Kudzu
- Oriental bittersweet
- Purple loosestrife
- Queen Anne's lace
- Tree-of-heaven

Not So Green Grasses

Weave motion and texture into your garden beds with perennial picks

1. Pink muhly grass

MUHLENBERGIA CAPILLARIS, ZONES 5 TO 9
Make room in the garden for this late-season standout. Muhly's pink flowers, followed by purplish seeds, add welcome color in fall when many annuals and perennials are past their peaks. Tolerant of heat, humidity, drought and salt, this plant grows 1 to 3 feet tall and is even more impressive when used en masse.
Why we love it: The native grass provides food and cover for birds, butterflies and other kinds of wildlife.

2. Blue oat grass

HELICTOTRICHON SEMPERVIRENS, ZONES 4 TO 8
Blue oat grass is an excellent choice for well-draining to dry soils in sunny to partly sunny locations. The arching blue-green leaves form a mound 2 feet tall and wide. Blue flowers appear in summer, then fade to brown. Combine this ornamental option with other drought tolerant annuals and perennials for easy watering.
Why we love it: Black walnut, drought, deer and pollution aren't an issue for this grass.

3. Switchgrass

PANICUM VIRGATUM, ZONES 3 TO 10
The birds, the butterflies and you will all love this garden addition. The clump-forming native grows up to 6 feet tall and prefers full sun and moist, well-draining soil. Shenandoah, Northwind, Heavy Metal and other cultivars provide a variety of size options, making this grass a perfect fit for most landscapes.
Why we love it: Finches like to snack on the seed heads. Skipper butterflies use the grass as a host plant.

4. Indiangrass

SORGHASTRUM NUTANS, ZONES 3 TO 9
Enjoy seasons of beauty when you grow Indiangrass. The 5-to-7-foot-tall plant has blue-green blades that turn gold in the fall and are topped with gold-bronze seed heads. It does self-seed, so it's best used in gardens with room for it to spread.
Why we love it: This drought tolerant native plant provides a great habitat for songbirds and game birds.

5. Tufted hair grass

DESCHAMPSIA CESPITOSA, ZONES 4 TO 9

Earth-toned flowers appear above mounds of this native grass's green leaves in early summer. The leaves turn gold in fall and keep their color and shape throughout winter. The Northern Lights cultivar's green-and-cream variegated leaves have a pinkish blush in spring.

Why we love it: A host plant for several butterflies, this grass thrives in full sun to part shade and in lots of soils.

6. Prairie dropseed

SPOROBOLUS HETEROLEPIS, ZONES 3 TO 9

A native grass, prairie dropseed is adaptable but grows best in full sun and well-draining soils. The tufts of fine leaves grow 2 feet tall and 3 feet wide and persist through winter. Fall flowers are followed by seed heads that look like gems when covered with ice. Use as a substitute for invasive fountain grass.

Why we love it: Forming a gorgeous carpet, it's at home in prairie or natural gardens.

7. Blue fescue

FESTUCA GLAUCA, ZONES 4 TO 8

Tolerant to heat, drought and salt, this is a great choice for those challenging conditions. Grow it as a companion alongside blanket flower, sedum and globe thistle. Avoid using it in areas with poor drainage. Blue fescue grows up to 1 foot tall and has silvery foliage that is evergreen in warmer climates.

Why we love it: Low growing and water wise, it makes a nice edger, ground cover or accent plant.

8

8. Feather reed grass

CALAMAGROSTIS SPP., ZONES 4 TO 9

This grass provides a vertical accent 3 to 5 feet tall in a garden, along a border or in a container. Though best in full sun to light shade and well-draining, moist soil, it can adapt. Black walnut, drought, deer and rabbits won't bother it.

Why we love it: Tall enough to command attention, it'll thrive even in small yards.

BEST SEDGES

These plants look like grass but thrive in shadowy spots.

- For dry to average soils: ivory sedge (Carex eburnea), long-beaked (C. sprengelii) and white-tinged (C. albicans).

- For moist to wet soils: blue sedge (C. glauca), eastern star (C. radiata) or gray (C. grayi).

---

9. Little bluestem grass

SCHIZACHYRIUM SCOPARIUM, ZONES 3 TO 10

It's no surprise this 3-foot-tall, drought tolerant native grass was selected as the 2022 Perennial Plant of the Year. Grow it in full sun and well-draining soil. Cultivars such as Jazz or Standing Ovation tend to stand upright and not flop in rich soils, and Prairie Winds Blue Paradise is deep wine purple in fall.

Why we love it: Fluffy silver-white seed heads last all through winter.

10. Japanese forest grass

HAKONECHLOA MACRA, ZONES 4 TO 9

Combine this shade-loving grass with hostas, coral bells and astilbes. Its fine texture looks fantastic in covered spots, with a growth habit that is reminiscent of a spider plant. Consistently moist and well-draining soil is a must. Grow in woodland and border gardens.

Why we love it: Variegated cultivars with white, green or gold striping offer even more appeal.

Show Off Your Succulents

Eight easy ways to make the water-saving plants stand out in the garden

A hollow log is a gorgeous DIY planter.

SUCCULENTS HAVE BEEN POPULAR HOUSEPLANTS FOR YEARS, and for good reason. They are easy to care for and come in a wide range of colors, shapes and sizes. Here are eight ways to let them shine outside.

1. Decorate a Fence
Top a fence or wall with planter boxes and let succulents such as burro's tail or string of pearls trail downward to soften the structure and add visual interest.

2. Make a Mosaic
With so much variety, succulents are ready to be mixed and matched into any design or pattern. Combine different types to create a mosaic. Be creative with your plants and arrangements. Geometric and abstract designs both look great. You can also throw in cactuses (which prefer the same growing conditions) for extra texture.

3. Arrange a Potted Vignette
Succulents do great in containers, but the plants are sometimes too small to carry visual interest from a distance. That's when it pays to group plants in color-coordinated vessels so they look like one cohesive unit. Repeat your chosen hue and mix up the heights and sizes of the pots for more appeal.

Angelina sedum

You can include a darker accent container to add depth.

4. Plant Ground Cover

Outdoor succulents make outstanding drought tolerant ground covers. Pick one that's hardy in your area—Angelina sedum or hens-and-chicks grow in many places. The plants save time and effort once they're established, and provide much more color and dimension to your landscape than traditional grass.

5. Create a Miniature Garden

Plant a miniature fairy garden to enjoy up close. Most of these gardens are small enough to be portable, so you can plant one in a container and move it wherever you want. Maybe it's a centerpiece for an outdoor party that later sits on the porch. Plus you can take it indoors to a bright and sunny location if cold weather is on the way.

6. Fill a Worry-Free Window Box

Sure, we've all forgotten to water a window box at some point. And we've all paid the price with dead— or at least mightily struggling— plants. Here's where succulents come to the rescue. They can go a week or more between waterings, depending on the conditions, so they'll still look fresh even if their irrigation is irregular for a spell.

7. Rock On With a Rock Garden

Succulents should be a part of every rock garden—if not the main attraction. They are naturally adapted to hot, sunny conditions and the lean soil of traditional rock gardens. Many succulents will creep and slowly

Mix different succulents for an eclectic centerpiece.

cover the stone, while others will stay small and fill little pockets.

8. Have a Ball

A precast concrete sphere with holes of various sizes can be filled with potting mix and an assortment of succulents. Similar products to the one shown below can be found in garden centers, or you can make your own. Drill holes into

a bowling ball or globe, or shape chicken wire and coco liner into a round planter.

A concrete sphere with sedum, Pachyphytum and elephant bush.

Ready for Heat

Fill your summer garden with water-wise picks

1

MULTIPLE BENEFITS
Beyond its ability to attract pollinators, amethyst sea holly is easy to grow and resists salt damage.

1. Amethyst sea holly

ERYNGIUM AMETHYSTINUM, ZONES 3 TO 9

Eye-catching and compact, sea holly has spiny gray-green foliage and prickly cool blue flower heads that bloom in mid-to-late summer. This deer-resistant plant loves hot sun and well-draining soil but will survive just about anywhere. Add this sea holly to borders or a cutting garden.

Why we love it: Bees and butterflies flock to this plant's blooms, which also shine in floral arrangements.

2. Moss rose

PORTULACA GRANDIFLORA, ANNUAL

A member of the purslane family, moss rose grows to create a mat that is 3 to 8 inches high and up to 1 foot wide. It makes for a stunning spiller in a hanging planter. Give it full sun—the flowers open only in sunlight before closing in the evening. Try the Fairy Tale series for pompomlike flowers or Sundial for blooms that stay open longer during the day.

Why we love it: The petals have a ruffled appearance and come in a wide array of colors.

3. Rosemary

SALVIA ROSMARINUS,
ZONES 7 TO 11 OR ANNUAL

A fragrant evergreen shrub that also serves as a savory herb, rosemary has needlelike leaves and clusters of flowers in pale blue to white that bloom from late winter through summer. Growing up to 6 feet tall, it requires moist, well-draining soil and full sun for best results. Prune if desired after flowering.

Why we love it: You can keep it in a pot indoors to overwinter or for easy additions to recipes.

4. Gold Nugget hens-and-chicks

SEMPERVIVUM, ZONES 4 TO 9

Provide a year-round display of vibrant color with Gold Nugget. The succulent's foliage changes from lime green in summer to golden red during cooler months. Place it in gritty, well-draining soil where the plant can receive full sun or very light shade.

Why we love it: With low-growing rosettes that spread 6 to 8 inches, hens-and-chicks can be easily divided by pulling out a few chicks (smaller rosettes) and replanting.

5. Pineleaf penstemon

PENSTEMON PINIFOLIUS, ZONES 4 TO 9

Native to the southern Rocky Mountains, this compact perennial features foliage that resembles pine needles and has tubular flowers with bright red, orange and yellow tones. Also known as beardtongue, penstemon loves full sun and is a magnet for bees, hummingbirds and other helpful pollinators.

Why we love it: Deer leave it alone. Plus it's easy to grow on slopes or in rock gardens.

6. Color Guard Adam's needle

YUCCA FILAMENTOSA, ZONES 4 TO 10

This desert plant has spiked variegated foliage and ivory bell-shaped flowers that appear on 4-to-6-foot stalks in midsummer. It's a striking focal point in a low-water garden. Put it in a spot with sunshine and well-draining soil, and this will easily grow 2 to 3 feet wide. Find it at an online retailer such as Monrovia.

Why we love it: Color Guard is salt tolerant, does well as a container plant and attracts hummingbirds, but deer tend to leave it be.

7. Red creeping thyme

THYMUS PRAECOX 'COCCINEUS', ZONES 3 TO 8

Creeping thyme is a drought tolerant ground cover with a bounty of blooms. Many thyme varieties do well with very little water, but this magenta-hued version is especially vibrant and fragrant. Keep it in full or part sun. Tuck clusters into rock gardens or near walls, where they will spread 8 to 12 inches.

Why we love it: The dark foliage slowly transforms to a beautiful bronze color during fall.

8. Butterfly weed

ASCLEPIAS TUBEROSA, ZONES 3 TO 9

This bushy perennial is known for its showstopping clusters of vivid flowers that bloom throughout the summer. Add it to a cottage garden with easy access for cut flowers. The seedpods add texture and interest to a dried floral arrangement, and it will self-seed if pods aren't removed.

Why we love it: Butterflies adore it and monarchs use it as a host plant.

9. Arizona Sun blanket flower

GAILLARDIA, ZONES 3 TO 9

Requiring little water and suitable in small spaces, this easy-to-grow perennial forms a swath of deep red, orange and yellow daisylike blossoms. Arizona Sun, an All-America Selections winner sold by Monrovia and other producers, prefers full sun and well-draining soil, and it beautifully tolerates heat.

Why we love it: A long-lasting bloomer, it flowers from early summer to fall. Deadhead to extend the color show.

WATER-WISE NATIVES

- Agave
- California lilac (Ceanothus)
- Prickly pear (Opuntia)
- Tarragon (Artemisia dracunculus)
- Trumpet vine (Campsis radicans)

10. Cascade stonecrop

SEDUM DIVERGENS, ZONES 2 TO 9

This succulent's tightly stacked, plump leaves range from green to darker red. Golden, star-shaped flowers appear in summer. Also known as spreading stonecrop, it's a tough, low-maintenance plant that needs lots of sunlight but very little water.

Why we love it: Use this fast-growing plant as a ground cover or to enhance rock gardens, borders and containers.

Carefree
and Cool

Coneflowers promise the novice grower low-maintenance care while enticing the experienced gardener with exciting cultivars that bloom from summer until frost

Kismet White
coneflower

POPULAR PERENNIALS NATIVE to central and eastern states, coneflowers are garden workhorses. They are known botanically as Echinacea, and they're self-seeders that spread every year to fill a garden with color, providing a reliable show when other flowers fade. They're also easy to control—simply pull any unwanted tender young seedlings that sprout in spring.

Beloved for their daisylike look that makes a big impact in the garden, coneflowers' blooms reach up to 4 inches wide. The are the perfect cutting flower for when your indoor space could benefit from a cheerful backyard bouquet.

Perfect for Pollinators
Savvy gardeners with green thumbs aren't coneflowers' only fans. Debbie Roos, an agriculture extension agent with the Chatham County Center of North Carolina Cooperative Extension designed and maintains a demonstration pollinator garden that includes more than 225 species of plants, 85% of them native to North Carolina. She's seen her share of coneflower visitors.

Monarch butterfly

MAKE THE CUT

Coneflowers last up to two weeks in an indoor bouquet. Even the seed heads look good once the petals drop.

Sombrero Salsa Red and Evolution Colorific coneflowers planted with Northwind switch grass.

PLAYS WELL WITH OTHERS
Coneflowers love company. Grow them with similar bloomers or even native grasses.

"Coneflowers provide nectar and pollen for many species, including bees, butterflies, flower flies and beetles," she says. "They are also important to birds. Hummingbirds enjoy the nectar and songbirds feed on the seeds from fall through winter if you leave the plants intact at the tail end of the growing season."

Debbie has also observed many bee species visiting coneflowers, including bumblebees, leafcutter bees, small carpenter bees, sweat bees, honeybees and others.

Coneflowers lure another beneficial flier that natural ecosystems rely on: butterflies. Debbie says they attract swallowtails, monarchs, American ladies, sulphurs and more. "They're also a host plant for silvery checkerspot butterflies," she adds.

Lovely Landscape Uses

As a native plant, coneflowers thrive in naturalized areas. Purple coneflower (Echinacea purpurea), the most popular and well-known of the bunch, is the best suited for natural environments because it tolerates dry conditions once established. In these settings, grow other prairie plants that complement coneflowers, such as black-eyed Susan, native grasses and yarrow.

Coneflowers' charm and grace also make them a standout in a cottage-style garden. With blooms perched on upright stems, this old-fashioned favorite mingles well with Shasta daisies, bee balm and garden phlox. Or plant with color in mind. Purple coneflower complements the bright orange hue of butterfly weed and enhances the pastel palette of plants such as silvery lamb's ear or pink verbena.

Grown en masse, they perform well in both borders and berms, promising endless drifts of color. Over time, they grow to create a lush look that requires only a little upkeep, such as occasional thinning. Grow coneflowers with equally assertive plant partners such as agastache or native grasses to add some diversity.

A Little TLC Goes a Long Way

Coneflowers do best in Zones 3 to 9, making them suitable for growing within most of the United States. While they can handle partial shade, plant them in full sun for maximum flower power. If planting from seed, sow after the danger of frost has passed (start indoors eight to 10 weeks before the last frost date to get a jump-start).

Another easy-care trait of coneflowers is that they adapt to a variety of soil conditions. Loose, well-draining soil is ideal, but most coneflowers will acclimate to rocky or clay soils over time. Although coneflowers are tolerant to both heat and drought, work compost into the ground around plants in early spring, water regularly through the growing season, and mulch in winter to keep plants strong and protected from common diseases like powdery mildew.

While it's true that these beauties generally have a low-fuss factor, some simple care keeps them healthy and thriving, especially when it comes to the flashy cultivars available at garden centers.

5 MUST-TRY CONEFLOWER CULTIVARS

Available in more colors than ever, this garden all-star comes in white, yellow, orange, pink and red.

1. WHITE SWAN
The snowy white petals of this garden classic wrap around a coppery cone for a natural look perfect for inclusion ofna native garden.

2. BIG KAHUNA
Add a tropical touch to a landscape with mango-hued blooms that boast a scent as lovely as the Hawaiian Islands.

3. HOT PAPAYA
Spicy red-orange flowers with a pompom center bloom from mid-to-late summer and pack a visual punch when planted in groups.

4. DOUBLE DECKER
The unusual two-tiered blooms feature cheerful dark pink petals that make garden visitors take a second look.

5. MELLOW YELLOWS
Bees and butterflies especially love the creamy, dreamy flowers that bloom from summer into late fall, offering a long-lasting show.

Creating Winter
Interest

Eight bold plants sure to provide a wonderland of color and beauty

◀ COTONEASTER

Bursting with bright red berries that last through winter, this deer resistant shrub thrives in cold, windy areas and withstands damage from salt spray. Use it to edge driveways or line retaining walls. With several species available, the options are endless.

▲ BOXWOOD

The workhorse of the winter garden, boxwood adds color and structure. Its natural form is pretty, or you can prune it into a flat hedge or round orb in spring. It also grows in containers. Winter Gem is a reliable beauty to consider.

Witch hazel brings colorful yellow flower clusters to chilly landscapes.

▲ WITCH HAZEL

It's low maintenance, resilient and ignored by most pests. In addition, it provides a wow factor with spidery flowers in hues of yellow, orange, red, copper and purple that bloom in fall or winter into early spring. Not only does this plant light up the dormant landscape, but it's fragrant, too. Grow it as a small tree or a large shrub.

▶ ORNAMENTAL GRASSES

Create intrigue in an otherwise barren garden with elegant stems and plumes that stand at attention and sway with a whisper of winter wind. Grasses also make a terrific source of shelter and food for songbirds. Plant them in masses for big impact and cut them back in early spring. Feather reed grass is a striking, sterile option.

Black-capped
chickadee

▲ CRABAPPLE

Best known for presenting a springtime show, these trees also produce red, orange and
yellow fruits that appear in fall and persist into winter. They offer a pop of color against
snowy gardens and provide food for birds. For a small yard, consider Tina or Firebird.
Both are disease resistant with vibrant fruits.

Beyond winter, red twig dogwood pops with flowers and berries in warmer months.

▲ RED TWIG DOGWOOD

With red branches that look like coral in a wintry sea, this cold-hardy native stuns. At home in woodland and rain gardens, it shines in every season. Cut old stems back in spring to optimize color on new growth.

Bohemian
waxwing

▲ MOUNTAIN ASH

Its red-orange berry clusters cling through winter and provide much-needed color against a gray sky. In fall, enjoy fernlike leaves that turn yellow to red before dropping. This native is tolerant of strong winds and serves as a vital food source for birds, especially hungry cedar and Bohemian waxwings.

▶ HARRY LAUDER'S WALKING STICK

This odd-shaped shrub is a conversation starter with bright yellow catkins that dangle from twisty branches. Plant it where everyone can appreciate its one-of-a-kind silhouette. Red twig dogwood is Rachael Liska's choice for easy, amazing color in a winter garden.

Red-bellied
woodpecker

CHAPTER 6

Butterfly Life

Discover how to identify and entice these delicate visitors

Zoom in on Butterflies

Photographing the fast fliers requires patience, but these snapshots from readers prove it's worth the wait

Most of the sunflowers in my New Jersey garden bloom in August. I also have abundant fresh milkweed, which invites monarch butterflies, on my property. One early afternoon, when the clouds provided some filter from the harsh sun, I photographed a monarch and a bumblebee on one of the sunflowers. I just love the combination of the butterfly, bee and flower together. The picture celebrates the height of the season.

Cheryl Fleishman
WANTAGE, NEW JERSEY

▲ This painted lady stopped and sunned itself on my hydrangeas for a long time. I got several wonderful shots using a Canon EOS Rebel T7.

Ashley Veatch
SEARCY, ARKANSAS

► A close-up look at this fiery skipper on a coneflower offers lots of details. I saw the tiny butterfly near the Calypso Cove Marina on Lake Thunderbird State Park in Norman, Oklahoma.

Stephen Ofsthun
NORMAN, OKLAHOMA

While my husband was busy at a meeting in Washington, D.C., my camera and I cruised the National Mall area. I came across a garden full of common buckeye butterflies. I loved how the orange lantana flowers complemented the butterflies' orange-tipped wings. This one sat patiently, watching me, for its photo shoot. I've upgraded my DSLR camera several times since, but this has remained one of my favorite butterfly photos.

Stephanie Young
PADUCAH, KENTUCKY

My wife and I like to vacation in the South, and on this particular trip we decided to go to Jekyll Island in Georgia. We went to Driftwood Beach to get some good photos of the area. To my surprise, hundreds of Gulf fritillaries were migrating along the coast—it was a bonus for me. I love the yellow lantana flowers and the angle of the butterfly in this shot.

Ron Punako
HOLLSOPPLE, PENNSYLVANIA

▶ **I had my** Nikon D500 in the backyard, hoping to capture a hooded oriole. When I saw this western tiger swallowtail butterfly land on my lilac, I had to laugh—because it's yellow and black, just like a male hooded oriole!

Della Alcorn
REDDING, CALIFORNIA

▼ **Out of the** corner of my eye I saw a small Ceraunus blue butterfly fluttering around tall weeds in an overgrown field. I used a photography technique called focus stacking to get as much of the butterfly in focus as possible. Luckily, one of my exposures captured its extended proboscis, the sippy straw it uses to extract nectar from flowers.

Stephan Barrett
SORRENTO, FLORIDA

9 Ways to Attract Butterflies

Make your garden the most popular stop around with expert tips and tricks

Bordered patch
butterfly on
firewheel
(Gaillardia
pulchella)

Gulf fritillary
on smooth
beggartick

Painted lady on
buttonbush

ANYONE CAN FILL A GARDEN with the vivid colors of delicate butterflies. Jaret Daniels, author of multiple butterfly field guides and associate professor at the McGuire Center for Lepidoptera and Biodiversity at the University of Florida's Museum of Natural History, offers his advice for getting more visitors.

1. Grow Local

Native plants are the perfect choice for a butterfly garden. "They are adapted to the local soils and climate," Jaret says. "As a result, they often perform better than nonnative species." You'll spend less money and effort to attract more butterflies in the long run.

"Natives often have the reputation of looking unkempt or weedy," Jaret says. "But there are many natives that are just as attractive as nonnative ornamentals." Visit a native plant nursery or contact your local county extension office to get a good list for your area.

2. Start with Nectar Favorites

Jaret recommends putting in a selection of popular nectar plants, then getting a good field guide to learn which butterfly species visit them the most. But don't go crazy and buy one of everything you see.

Black swallowtail
emerging from
chrysalis

Sunflowers provide nectar for butterflies, such as monarchs, and seeds for birds.

Monarch caterpillars on butterfly weed

"The kid-in-a-candy-store approach may not yield the best results," says Jaret. "Instead, select several really good plants and buy a few of each. The larger waves of color help draw in insects." Include plants of varying heights, and don't neglect shady spots—some butterflies prefer them.

3. Add Host Plants

Once you've identified the butterflies visiting your yard, add the host plants that their caterpillars need. Each species has its own requirements. For instance, monarchs use milkweed, while eastern black swallowtails eat from the parsley family. Once again, natives reign supreme, so choose local species of milkweed and other hosts for the most success.

4. Create a Caterpillar Haven

It usually takes about two weeks for a caterpillar to reach full size. Then it spends 10 to 14 days as a chrysalis before emerging as a butterfly. "Most adult butterflies live only a few short weeks," Jaret says. "The other life stages actually reside in your garden much longer and are just as attractive and entertaining."

Of course, all butterfly gardeners should avoid using pesticides altogether. Find alternative ways to deal with true pests, such as picking them off by hand, which helps keep caterpillars safe.

5. Offer Shelter

A butterfly weighs about as much as a paper clip, so to them a raindrop can feel like a bowling ball. They seek shelter in bad weather and overnight, often in shrubbery or ornamental grasses, or tucked into cracks in rock piles. Provide these spaces for extra security.

6. Treasure Your Trees

You may picture sunny meadows when thinking of butterflies, but plenty of species, such as red-spotted purples and white admirals, prefer shade. In the spring, running tree sap provides some of the earliest butterfly meals. A few trees serve as host plants, too. For example, tiger swallowtail caterpillars use cottonwood, birch and black cherry trees as nurseries.

7. Serve Sweets

Many butterflies enjoy fruit in addition to (or instead of) nectar from flowers. Grow native berry-producing shrubs or fruit trees, allowing the fruit to drop to the ground naturally. As it rots, the fruit becomes a draw for species such as red admirals and mourning cloaks. If you see a lot of fruit lovers, try setting out a plate of overripe bananas or juicy options such as oranges or watermelon. Beware—this can also attract raccoons and other pests, so bring the fruit plate in at night.

8. Protect Puddles

Male butterflies like to cluster on mud puddles (or you may find them on animal dung or roadkill), where they glean valuable salts and minerals. It's hard to create these spots artificially, so if you have a popular muddy area in your garden, leave it be. The butterflies will thank you.

9. Appreciate Your Space

Whether you have a huge lot or a tiny balcony, you can attract butterflies. "A butterfly garden can be any size," says Jaret. "Small beds or container gardens with a combination of colorful nectar plants and a larval host plant or two can be quite effective."

Jaret shares a final thought: "My theme for the past few years has been 'all landscapes matter.' With habitat loss, the landscapes that we as humans manage every day are increasingly important to wildlife. So the choices we make in our home gardens really matter.

Attract black swallowtails with drought-tolerant yellow coneflowers.

Raising Monarchs

These orange-and-black insects are a joy to observe as they hatch from eggs, grow into caterpillars and transform into butterflies. Here's a collection of reader photos and stories about watching the next generation take flight.

Monarch caterpillar

◄ **My daughter Addison** was diagnosed with Type 1 diabetes and admitted to the hospital for three days. It came as a shock but, thankfully, with insulin and the correct treatment, she bounced back quickly. Although diabetes is a scary diagnosis, Addison adjusted like a pro and does her injections and blood draws almost completely independently. Her bright, vibrant smile is back and she feels awesome. We did a mini photo shoot as we said goodbye to a group of the monarchs we raised. Every year we raise as many as we can to help their dwindling population. It is such a satisfying experience to watch their amazing life cycle and even more rewarding to share it with my daughter.

Brianne Colling
CANTON, MICHIGAN

► **This little one** was so new it hadn't yet let go of its chrysalis. We do everything we can to encourage butterflies to visit, such as planting milkweed, zinnia and other favorites. In 2020, we were blessed with 36 monarch caterpillars and 32 found chrysalises. We watch migration charts and hope for another good year.

Arnold Leuenberger
JONESBOROUGH, TENNESSEE

▲ **I have a large pot** filled with milkweed that attracts monarchs. The caterpillars go crazy feeding on the plant, but I had never seen a chrysalis until last summer when I found one on a nearby ponytail palm. I took this photo just a few hours before the butterfly emerged. At last, success! A female monarch butterfly flew away to start the cycle all over again.

Trudy Peterson
DAVENPORT, FLORIDA

▶ **I snapped this photo** of a monarch a few summers ago after I placed a tag on its wings. This one stopped to pose nicely before its long journey to Mexico.

Jessica Bisko
MORRISDALE, PENNSYLVANIA

WATCHING MIGRATION
Monarch Watch is a citizen science project in which volunteers place sticker tags on monarchs' wings to help scientists track the butterflies' migration patterns. To learn more or get involved, go to monarchwatch.org.

This photo is from the first year that I raised monarch butterflies from caterpillars or, as my granddaughter calls them, "callipitters." These butterflies were the first to emerge from their chrysalises. It was more than magical!

Susan Blake
THIENSVILLE, WISCONSIN

Monarch caterpillars on milkweed

A butterfly kit is a great way to teach kids about life cycles.

HOW TO HELP MONARCHS

Here are some simple ways you can protect these beautiful butterflies.

SKIP PESTICIDES
The common sprays harm butterflies. Try to use pest control methods without chemicals.

PLANT A POLLINATOR GARDEN
Patches of flowers help fuel monarchs on their long migrations.

JOIN A CITIZEN SCIENCE PROJECT
Journey North, Project Monarch Health and Monarch Watch are among numerous ways to get involved.

GROW MILKWEED
It's the only plant that monarch caterpillars will eat.

Spotted in the South

Look for white peacocks year-round in wetlands and fields

CHECK IT OUT!
Look for one dark spot on forewings and two on hindwings.

▲ I captured this image in the heat of summer at a local nature center in southwest Michigan. I love photographing butterflies from different perspectives, especially from beneath when I can see their faces. Each one is so uniquely beautiful and intricate.

Marguerite Eichelberger
BERRIEN SPRINGS, MICHIGAN

◄ While visiting the Desert Botanical Garden in Phoenix, Arizona, I saw this white peacock and several other species I had never seen before. Having so many different butterflies fluttering around was a wondrous experience.

Deborah Billings
WATKINSVILLE, GEORGIA

White peacock caterpillars are dark with tiny white flecks throughout the body, in addition to intimidating spines used to scare off potential predators.

WHITE PEACOCK

WINGSPAN
2 to 2¾ inches.

DISTINCTIVE MARKINGS
White wings with brown markings and subtle orange hues along edges. Appears more pale in winter.

RANGE
The Southeast, as far west as Texas and north as North Carolina. Occasionally spotted in northern states during warmer months.

HABITAT
Along rivers, ponds and swampy areas, and in fields.

HOST PLANTS
Water hyssop, frogfruit and wild petunia.

EGGS
Green, underneath plant leaves.

ATTRACT THEM
Plant bidens and frogfruit to attract white peacocks.

Early Emergers

Adult mourning cloaks are among the first to exit hibernation

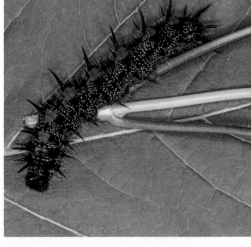

This striking caterpillar's black body sports large red patches along the top and tiny white dots all over, with dramatic spikes, called scoli, on its back and sides.

◀ **Mourning cloak** butterflies hatched like crazy last spring. I took this photo of a newly emerged butterfly just before it took its maiden flight.

Lisa Spruill
LOS ANGELES, CALIFORNIA

▶ **I captured this** shot of a mourning cloak getting nectar from a coneflower in my garden. The mourning cloaks seem to like an area with dead leaves, tree stumps and branch piles.

Brenda Doherty
ARISS, ONTARIO

MOURNING CLOAK

WINGSPAN
2¼ to 4 inches.

DISTINCTIVE MARKINGS
Dark maroon wings feature yellow speckling on the leading edge and a yellow band on the outer portion of the wing. Blue dots run along the band.

RANGE
Northern Canada to Guatemala, plus Europe and Asia.

HABITAT
Banks of streams, woods, parks and suburbs.

HOST PLANTS
Willows, poplars, elms and other trees.

ATTRACT THEM
Tree sap and decaying fruit are more appealing to adults than flower nectar.

Flights of Fancy

Painted lady butterflies rival monarchs in their migratory journeys

Painted ladies are mostly orange and brown with black and white accents.

WHEN YOU THINK OF BUTTERFLY MIGRATION, it's probably monarch butterflies that first spring to mind. Their epic journey to Mexico each year has caught the public's imagination, especially as their overwintering grounds have become threatened. But monarchs aren't the only butterflies that travel long distances. The painted lady also migrates, and its journey can be even more spectacular.

One of the most widespread butterflies in the world, the painted lady is commonly found in North America, Europe, Africa and Asia. In the United States, its range stretches from coast to coast, from sea level to mountains and valleys. Adults feed on flower nectar, while their caterpillars eat a huge variety of host plants, including thistles and mallows. They're unable to withstand freezing temperatures, so when winter comes, painted ladies need to find warmer climates.

"In North America, most painted ladies overwinter in Mexico," says Jaret Daniels, who has a doctorate in entomology and is an associate professor at the University of Florida. "Monarchs also overwinter there, but in only a few small areas of mountain forest." Painted ladies are much more spread out, preferring drier, warmer climates.

Unlike the monarch, the painted

A group of migrating painted ladies visit a field of mustard plants.

lady reproduces throughout its migrations. "Painted ladies breed along the fall migration back south," says Jaret. "By contrast, migrating fall monarchs typically do not breed." This means that wherever they are, painted ladies need access to the host plants their caterpillars eat throughout the year.

Painted ladies return north in the spring, breeding and spreading out to recolonize the United States. Their numbers are erratic and reflect the seasonal conditions. "In good-weather years, there can be huge numbers," Jaret says. "In bad-weather years, usually those with poor rainfall, their numbers are lower."

Heavy rains (often caused by El Niño weather patterns) can spark large wildflower blooms in painted ladies' desert wintering grounds. During these conditions, the painted lady migration is an incredible sight. Low-flying clouds of the butterflies appear in gardens, along highway medians or wherever their favorite nectar plants are found. They travel in waves so large that they're sometimes even seen on weather radars. These years are known as irruption years. During this time, painted ladies become even more widespread. This explains why some areas of the country, especially in the East, see painted ladies some years but not others.

Gardeners can easily support these butterflies throughout their journey. "Fuel is key," Jaret says. "Plant a diverse array of blooming plants that offer reliable nectar. Since painted ladies also breed along their route, provide host plants, too." With these easy steps, you'll help painted lady migrations stay strong and abundant for years to come.

AMAZING FLIGHT FACTS

- Painted ladies can fly at speeds close to 30 miles per hour and cover up to 100 miles in a day.
- These butterflies have been found at altitudes as high as 22,000 feet, the highest of any butterfly species.
- European painted ladies migrate to Africa in fall, crossing the Mediterranean and often continuing across the Sahara Desert. Their offspring then return north to Europe in spring.

Seek Red-Spotteds

Find these iridescent butterflies near streams or woods

I took this photo of a red-spotted purple butterfly at Kellys Run Nature Preserve in Holtwood, Pennsylvania. It's one of my favorite places to hike. I used a Tokina macro lens on a Nikon D5200 camera.

Nevin Shrom
PHILADELPHIA, PENNSYLVANIA

Discovering a new variety of butterfly in your garden is really exciting. This red-spotted purple butterfly looked gorgeous fluttering around our blooming purple coneflowers.

Mike Brickl
DOUSMAN, WISCONSIN

Red-spotted purple caterpillar

The brown, green and white caterpillars have humps on their backs and hornlike appendages.

RED-SPOTTED PURPLE

WINGSPAN
3 to 3½ inches.

DISTINCTIVE MARKINGS
From above, mostly black and iridescent blue with small orange spots on the wing tips. More red-orange markings from below.

RANGE
Eastern United States with additional populations in the Southwest.

HABITAT
Wooded areas—commonly found in suburbs.

HOST PLANTS
Cottonwoods, willows, wild cherries and other trees.

FAVORITE FOODS
Serve overripe bananas, citrus, apples or any other juicy fruit.

Black Beauty

Host black swallowtails with as little as a pot of herbs

My eyes were drawn to a black swallowtail moving from one flower to the next. I love the combination of black and purple that the butterfly and bloom created in this photo.

Joe Bob Hall
HOLLY LAKE RANCH, TEXAS

I've raised butterflies since the 1980s, but I never stop being amazed by their perfection as they emerge from the chrysalis.

Teresa Lee
TYRONE, GEORGIA

A caterpillar picked a fancy coneflower umbrella to begin its change into a black swallowtail butterfly in my backyard.

Aaron Hamilton
DENISON, TEXAS

The youngest caterpillars are nearly all black with a white back patch and orange spots. As they grow, they become mostly green with black bands and yellow markings.

BLACK SWALLOWTAIL

WINGSPAN
2¾ to 3¼ inches.

DISTINCTIVE MARKINGS
Primarily black from above, males have an extra band of yellow dots. Their bodies are also black with rows of yellow dots.

RANGE
East of the Rocky Mountains and parts of the Southwest.

HABITAT
Open areas such as gardens or wetlands.

HOST PLANTS
Celery, dill, parsley, sweet fennel and caraway.

EGGS
Perfectly round, yellow and found on many garden host plants.

On the Mark

Simple ways to identify and attract these gorgeous butterflies

Rust orange to yellow branching spines covering the body is the best clue for identification. Also look for a black body littered with tiny white and yellow dots arranged in a somewhat linear pattern.

▲ **I thought this** butterfly was a leaf! It's called a question mark because of the white markings on its wings.

Mary Gabriel
TUNKHANNOCK, PENNSYLVANIA

◀ **This is an infrequent** visitor to our backyard butterfly bushes. But working at home allowed me to see and photograph the beautiful question mark butterfly, providing a silver lining to the pandemic. The brilliant orange topside of its wings is a dramatic contrast to the underside, which perfectly mimics a dead leaf. Consequently, this butterfly is easily overlooked if its wings are closed.

Thomas Wetmore
SILVER SPRING, MARYLAND

▲ **I was on the porch** with my dear granddaughter Ava when we saw this newly emerged question mark as it dried its wings. When Ava lay down to get a closer look, the butterfly simply climbed on to her hand. This photo captures the wonders of nature through the eyes of a fascinated child. If we could all see like this, imagine the joy we could experience.
Rebecca May
WATERMAN, ILLINOIS

QUESTION MARK

WINGSPAN
2 to 2½ inches.

MARKINGS
Dark orange and black with spots on top, but more orange in winter. Brown and tan underneath, with long wing tips and the signature question marks on the wings.

RANGE
Throughout the eastern U.S. to the Rockies and into southern Canada.

HABITAT
Common in populated areas such as parks and backyards, as well as woodland clearings and streams.

EGGS
Green with vertical ridges.

HOST PLANTS
Hops, nettles, elms and hackberries.

CHAPTER 7

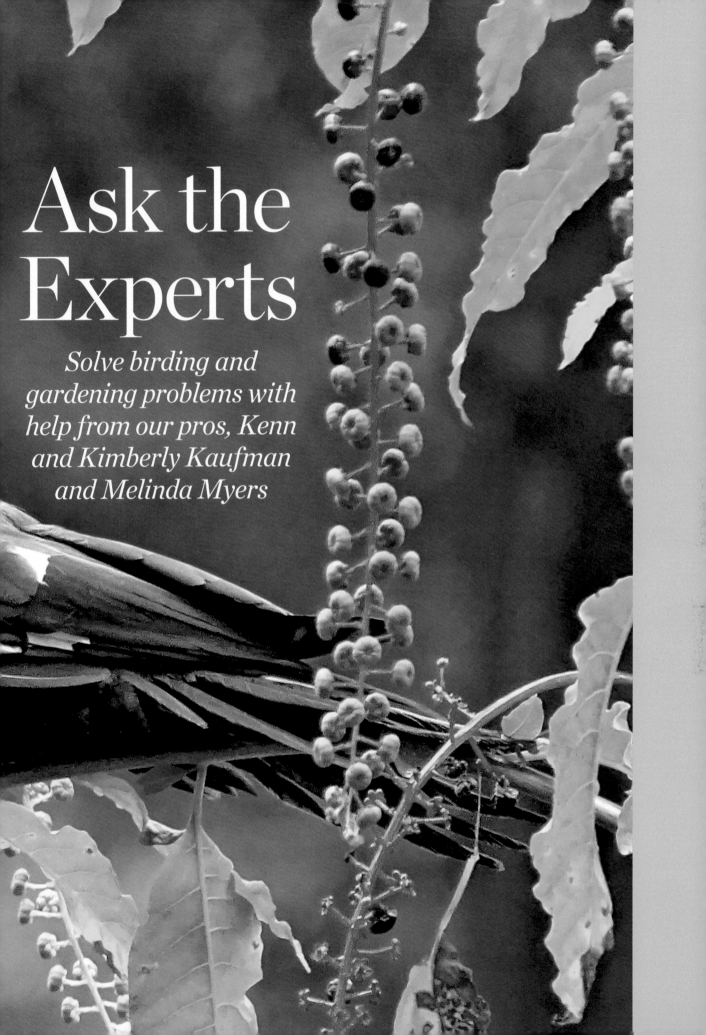

Ask the Experts

Solve birding and gardening problems with help from our pros, Kenn and Kimberly Kaufman and Melinda Myers

Cedar waxwing
on holly

Q Which holly tree is best for attracting birds?

David Caccia HAMMONTON, NEW JERSEY

Melinda: First make sure you have the right growing conditions for hollies and enough room for at least one male for every one to five female plants. Without both, the female plants won't produce berries. Hollies prefer moist, acidic soil, and evergreen hollies need shelter from winter's cold winds and bright sun, both of which can have a drying effect. American holly (*Ilex opaca*) is native and may be a good choice. It's a large tree that serves as a host for several caterpillars, and birds adore the berries. Or consider the deciduous winterberry (*Ilex verticillata*), a shrub that grows between 3 and 12 feet tall. It's hardy in Zones 3 to 9 and loses its leaves in winter, revealing berry-covered branches.

Q Last December I saw a Baltimore oriole at my feeders. Is that normal?

Ronald Boucher ROCHESTER, MASSACHUSETTS

Kenn and Kimberly: At one time, the answer would have been a flat no, because this species usually flew to tropical or subtropical regions in fall. But in recent years, more and more Baltimore orioles have been spending the winter at feeders in the eastern states. Most of them are south of your area—many winter in the Carolinas, for example—but now some survive the season as far north as Massachusetts almost every winter. A few have been noticed even farther north, in Maine or parts of southern Canada. So your December visitor is rare, but not unprecedented.

Q This bird is similar to several sparrows, but it doesn't seem to match any exactly. What is it?

Colleen Gibbs COON RAPIDS, MINNESOTA

Kenn and Kimberly: With a beautiful, clear photo such as yours, we have plenty of clues to check. This bird is a Lincoln's sparrow, an uncommon species in your area that is often shy. Its colors are helpful for checking its identity. The face is mostly gray, with reddish brown stripes along the sides of the crown, a buff mustache mark and a narrow buff eye ring. The chest is also buff with narrow black streaks. The bold black spot on the chest might be confusing since that's sometimes considered a field mark for song sparrows, but many other sparrows can show it.

Q Our son loves birds but has a severe peanut and tree nut allergy. What are some nut-free ways to feed visitors?

Christine Capriolo MILWAUKEE, WISCONSIN

Kenn and Kimberly: In colder months when raw suet won't turn rancid, this high-energy treat attracts woodpeckers, nuthatches, chickadees and other birds. Ask for a nut-free suet at the grocery store's meat counter. In warm weather, put out sliced fruit or jelly to attract orioles. Another option is to grow native or noninvasive plants. Instead of buying sunflower seeds, which may be produced in places that also handle nuts, plant sunflowers and leave them standing. You'll create a bonanza for finches and other birds. Nectar-rich plants and hummingbird feeders filled with sugar water safely attract those flying gems, too.

Q How do you tell male and female black-capped chickadees apart?

Hannah and Lily Ashdown
SCHUYLERVILLE, NEW YORK

Kenn and Kimberly: Male and female black-capped chickadees look identical, at least to humans, so behavioral clues are the only ways to distinguish them. It's mostly males that sing the signature *fee-bee* song. In aggressive encounters at bird feeders, males are usually dominant over females. During courtship, a male will feed his mate. Both members of a pair hollow out a cavity in a tree, then the female builds a nest inside and incubates the eggs. After the eggs hatch, the male brings most of the food to the nest, while the female tends to the hatchlings.

Black-capped chickadee

Q What are these white flowers? They grow from a large bulb and close during the night.

Wendy Gelnett MILLERSTOWN, PENNSYLVANIA

Melinda: This dainty spring bloomer is a star of Bethlehem (*Ornithogalum umbellatum*). It rapidly spreads through gardens into nearby lawns and, in some cases, natural areas. Digging the large bulbs is tedious, but it's the most effective way of managing the spread of this plant.

Q What's the best time to plant early-spring seeds?

Connie Etter MARTINSVILLE, INDIANA

Melinda: Check the back of the seed packet. Many have maps showing the best time to plant the seeds in your region, while others recommend spring planting dates based on the average last spring frost. You can find the average last spring and first fall frost dates on various websites, including most state university extension service sites. For your home in Indiana, Purdue University has a helpful online publication called the Indiana Vegetable Planting Calendar, which includes average frost dates.

Q Is this a house finch, a common redpoll or a purple finch?

Lynette Lozinski
ST. CLOUD, MINNESOTA

Kenn and Kimberly: Little red finches can be tricky. This bird has too much red to be a common redpoll—that tiny finch has just a little red cap and pink on the chest. Purple finches and house finches are more similar in appearance, as males of both have a lot of red on the head. This is a house finch. In your photo, the bird is perched at an angle, making it hard to discern the slimmer body, longer tail and slightly smaller bill of the house finch. But a good field mark here is the brown streaking along the sides and under the wings, which would be faint or lacking on a purple finch.

Q Bluebirds moved into the birdhouse I put out in spring. However, sparrows kept trying to nest in it. What should I do?

Steve Voelker FORT WAYNE, INDIANA

Kenn and Kimberly: The nonnative house sparrows compete with bluebirds for the same kinds of nesting sites. If you monitor the situation and clean out the sparrow nest every time they start to build, they may get discouraged and stop trying. It may help if you stop filling bird feeders during the time in spring when bluebirds are setting up their territories, because house sparrows don't stick around where there isn't an easy food source.

Eastern bluebirds

Q What's your favorite suet recipe?

Diane Mlekush MCHENRY, ILLINOIS

Kenn and Kimberly: We haven't settled on a favorite recipe because we're always experimenting. We always begin with equal parts lard and peanut butter, melting and mixing them over low heat. We add a variety of ingredients to this gooey mess, such as peanuts, raisins, rolled oats and cornmeal. (Avoid bacon grease, bread and table scraps.) Then we chill the mixture before cutting it into blocks or cubes. We check it regularly to be sure it isn't moldy or rancid.

Q Is this American robin leucistic?

Candy Brus GRAND RAPIDS, MICHIGAN

Kenn and Kimberly: Yes, this is a good example of the effects of leucism on a bird's plumage. This robin isn't a true albino, because it has dark eyes, a bright yellow bill and some areas of normal gray and orange rufous in its feathers. But it's lacking most of the pigment in its plumage, creating this striking, mostly white bird. Leucism occurs regularly in American robins, but it's a rare and special experience any time you get to see one like this.

Common
grackle

Q Common grackles consistently throw birdseed and empty my feeders. How can I deter them?

Stefanie Vanderbush WAUPUN, WISCONSIN

Kenn and Kimberly: To deal with the big appetites and messy habits of grackles, the best approach is to switch to different styles of feeders. Hanging tube-style feeders with short perches will attract finches and other small birds, but grackles find them hard to use. A suet feeder that can be accessed only from the underside will work for chickadees, nuthatches and other acrobatic birds, but may discourage grackles. You can also place a wire cage around a feeder—use wire with openings too small for grackles to squeeze through but big enough to let in finches, chickadees, juncos and other small birds.

Q My dog likes to do his "business" on my shrubs and flowers. Will this harm the plants?

Lona Shelters ELLENBURG CENTER, NEW YORK

Melinda: You may have noticed brown spots in your lawn from dog feces and urine, which contain nitrogen. If the concentration is high enough, it can burn your plants just like an excessive application of fertilizer. To avoid damage, remove the feces from garden spaces and wash urine off prized plants with water from a hose—this will also dilute it as it enters the soil.

Q. A cardinal pecks at my windows constantly. How do I make it stop?

Kay Baker MERCER, PENNSYLVANIA

Kenn and Kimberly: When a bird pecks at windows like that, it has mistaken its own reflection for another bird and is trying to drive it away. Some individuals become obsessed with these phantom rivals and may attack them for weeks. The only real solution is to do away with the reflection itself. Try rubbing a bar of soap on the outside of your windows in all the spots that the bird visits regularly. The cardinal should lose its drive to defend its territory after the breeding season wanes, so even if you can't block all the reflections, this behavior should end after a few weeks.

Q. A mourning dove built a nest near my front door. How long until the eggs hatch?

Aspasia Simeone
LONG BEACH, NEW YORK

Kenn and Kimberly: Mourning doves often choose protected spots on the ledges of houses for their twiggy nests. After the pair finishes building the nest—which takes two to four days—the female usually lays the first egg within a couple of days and a second egg a day or two later. Both parents will take turns incubating the two eggs. The eggs hatch after 14 days. Both adults feed the little ones, who will be ready to fly in about two weeks.

Q. What's the best way to encourage flower seedlings in my garden and discourage Bermuda grass?

Nathan Lembke BENTONVILLE, ARKANSAS

Melinda: It's certainly challenging to manage grass in an existing garden. Preemergent weed killers will prevent many desirable flower seeds, as well as weed seeds, from sprouting. Instead, continue to remove the Bermuda grass by hand. Spot treating the Bermuda grass plants with a total vegetation killer is another option, but be sure to protect desirable plants from these chemicals. You can cover a weed with a milk jug or soda bottle with the bottom removed, then spray the weed killer through the container's opening and onto the weed. Once dry, move to the next weed. Organic products only kill the above-ground portion of a plant, but repeated application can help manage this plant. Read and follow the label directions to make sure the product you select can be used in an existing garden.

Sunflower seedling

Q Bluebirds stay in a house in our yard year-round and raise several broods. When should we clean the house?

Bonnie Uhlenbrock GRIFFIN, GEORGIA

Kenn and Kimberly: While some bluebirds migrate to warmer climates in fall, many stay in the same place all year, especially in the South. They often roost in nest boxes during winter, as yours are doing, huddled together for added warmth on chilly nights. But being a responsible nest-box host means keeping them clean. Bluebird experts suggest cleaning them out after each brood has fledged. If that isn't possible, the boxes should be cleaned out after the last brood has left the nest in late summer. That timing won't disturb them or drive them away.

Q What kind of feeders can I add to my apartment balcony without making a mess?

Katie Schick BLUE BELL, PENNSYLVANIA

Kenn and Kimberly: Choosing the right food is the first step. Nuts, sunflower hearts and suet all create less mess. Visit a bird-feeding specialty store and ask about no-mess feeders that work well in your area. These options have trays that attach below the feeder to capture any debris. A saucer-style hummingbird feeder, which helps discourage bees and wasps, is another good option; make sure it has an ant moat to prevent ants.

Q An eerie silence fell over the usual bird chatter in my yard. Then I saw this hawk. What kind is it?

Pam Welsh BATON ROUGE, LOUISIANA

Kenn and Kimberly: The slim shape, short wings and long tail indicate that this is a member of the accipiter group of hawks, known for catching small birds. This one is a young sharp-shinned hawk, the smallest accipiter in North America. The young Cooper's hawk is similar, but has a bigger head and stripes on the chest that are usually narrower and darker. Adults of either species would have blue-gray backs and horizontal reddish bars on the chest.

Eastern bluebird

Cottontail rabbit

Q How do I keep bunnies from eating my flowers?

Maria Carreno ABSECON, NEW JERSEY

Melinda: Fencing and repellents are often used to prevent animal damage. A 4-foot-tall fence, anchored tightly to the ground and securely gated, is the most effective option. You can also try applying homemade or commercial repellents before rabbits or other animals begin feeding, repeating as recommended to increase success. Consider products (such as Plantskydd) that are rain and snow resistant, which extends the time between applications. Scare tactics are not always effective, especially in urban areas, as rabbits and other wildlife have grown accustomed to the sight and smell of humans. Continue to monitor your garden for damage and adjust strategies as needed.

Q Baltimore orioles came to my feeder minutes after I set it up. How did they find it so quickly?

Nancy Schanda SPRINGFIELD, MISSOURI

Kenn and Kimberly: We are often surprised at how rapidly birds show up when feeders are put out for the first time. Many kinds of birds seem to have developed an image in their minds of what certain types of feeders look like, and they recognize them even at a distance. In the case of your oriole visitors, they probably were somewhere nearby, even if you hadn't seen them—they can be very inconspicuous among the foliage of trees—so it didn't take them long to notice the feeders. Wild birds in general are highly observant of changes in their surroundings, especially those that involve potential food sources.

Q. How do caterpillars secure their chrysalises to a wall like this?

Carolyn Krause SAN ANTONIO, TEXAS

Kenn and Kimberly: Most caterpillars are able to spin silken threads from glands on their heads. On a raised surface such as this wall, the larva spins a pad of sticky silk and attaches to it while transforming into the chrysalis. Many chrysalises simply hang from where they're attached. But swallowtail butterfly chrysalises, such as the pipevine swallowtail's seen here, are held in an upright position by a thin thread just above the middle of the chrysalis.

Q. My forsythia had flowers for the past two years, but only on the bottom of the shrub. What's wrong with it?

Janet Grosse MADISON, WISCONSIN

Melinda: This is a common problem for those of us growing forsythia in colder climates. Even though the plant tolerates the winter cold, the dormant flower buds that form during the previous summer are often killed. In the future, select forsythia cultivars, such as Meadowlark, Northern Gold, Northern Sun, Show Off Starlet, Gold Cluster or Fiesta. They all have hardy flower buds that can withstand colder weather.

Forsythia

Q What's the best way to fertilize a blue spruce during spring?

Jennifer Broadstreet Hess MARION, KANSAS

Melinda: Trees and shrubs obtain most of their nutrients from grass clippings left on the lawn, organic mulch as it decomposes and fertilizer applied to surrounding garden beds. Have your soil tested to ensure you apply the right type and amount of fertilizer for the results you want. Otherwise, if you skip the testing, use a low-nitrogen, slow-release fertilizer before growth begins in spring. This type of fertilizer encourages balanced growth (both above and below the ground) that is more drought tolerant and resistant to insects, pests and disease. The fertilizer label often lists these attributes and provides information on how to apply it.

Q Why do ruby-throated hummingbirds' red feathers appear black at times?

Steven Hogan BIGLERVILLE, PENNSYLVANIA

Kenn and Kimberly: The beautiful iridescent colors of some hummingbird feathers have a surprising source. The feather itself may be a dull blackish color, but it's covered with a thin layer of clear cells that are structured to reflect light only in certain ways, as a prism does. Light striking the feather from just the right angle reflects back brilliant red, violet or green, depending on the species. The color can shift as the angle changes, which is why a ruby-throated's neck sometimes may look gold or greenish. But without direct lighting, those feathers simply look black.

Male ruby-throated hummingbird at coral honeysuckle vine

Firefly Peach
Sky yarrow

Q Most of my yarrow flower stems flopped over. What happened?

Douglas Tracy POMFRET CENTER, CONNECTICUT

Melinda: Yarrow prefers well-draining soil and is drought tolerant once established. It tends to grow tall and flop in moist and rich soil, hot weather or when too much nitrogen fertilizer is applied. You can adjust your care to promote more compact growth and prevent the stems from falling over. Just prune the plants back by one third after the first set of flowers fade. Then cut back new growth near the base of the plant after the second flush of flowers finish their show. Or you can cut the stems halfway to the ground when they are about 18 inches tall and before the first flowers appear. Consider providing some structural support for the plant by surrounding it with sturdier plants.

Q I found milkweed tiger caterpillars on my milkweed plants. Can they harm monarchs?

Karen Funk HILLMAN, MICHIGAN

Kenn and Kimberly: The milkweed tiger or milkweed tussock moth (*Euchaetes egle*) looks most interesting in its larval stage. The caterpillar is festooned with tufts of black, white and yellow-orange hairs. The adult moth is much plainer, with unmarked pale gray or brown wings. Several kinds of insects feed on milkweeds, and none will harm monarch caterpillars directly. Some can become so numerous that they reduce the amount of food available for the monarchs, but that seldom happens with milkweed tiger moths. If you're worried, the solution is just to plant more milkweed.

Q How do I prevent hummingbirds from flying into my sliding glass door?

Wendy Haste EAST PEORIA, ILLINOIS

Kenn and Kimberly: Along with roaming cats, window strikes are among the leading causes of bird deaths. Because glass reflects the outside scenery, birds think they can fly through. To prevent strikes, you must break up the reflection on the outside of the glass. Decals pasted on the inside of windows (hawk silhouettes are a common choice) are not enough to protect birds. However, peoples' growing awareness of window strikes has led to several fantastic products coming onto the market. We have tried BirdTape from the American Bird Conservancy and found it to be highly effective.

Q What's this bird?

Julie Konetzki SOUTH ELGIN, ILLINOIS

Kenn and Kimberly: The most unusual thing about this bird is the fact that you took a good photo of it! This is a blue-gray gnatcatcher. It's such a tiny, active sprite that it's always a challenge for photographers. But blue-gray gnatcatchers are widespread in summer in the forests of the eastern U.S. and the Southwest, and they spend winter in the southernmost states and Mexico. They are recognized by their small size, blue-gray back, white eye ring and long tail with white outer feathers.

Q My plant lost the pattern on its leaves. Is there anything I can do to get it back?

Wanda Bankey MILES CITY, MONTANA

Melinda: What you're experiencing is a relatively common occurrence with certain variegated plants, which are plants that display distinct patterns on their foliage. A branch or more may mutate back to the original green. The all-green shoots will be more vigorous than the variegated portion of the plant. To help maintain the plant's overall variegated look, prune out the green stems as they appear. If your whole plant has lost its variegation, you may be stuck with a slightly less interesting plant. In that case, you can either embrace it or replace it with a different option.

Nana Variegata weigela

ODD SPOTS
Carolina wrens aren't very picky about where they build nests and can choose places such as flower pots or hanging baskets. In this case, the bird made a home within a mop.

Q Is this how hummingbirds sleep?
Sarah Latimer
CAMBRIDGE SPRINGS, PENNSYLVANIA

Kenn and Kimberly: Although it isn't their normal position, hummingbirds do sometimes sleep upside down. The tiny birds have a rapid metabolism and risk burning up most of their energy while they sleep. So they may go into a condition called torpor, in which their heartbeat, breathing and other bodily functions slow way down to conserve energy. When they sleep, their toes close tightly around their perch. If it's a smooth branch, they may slip until they're hanging downward. It looks alarming, but this bird should be able to right itself when it wakes up.

Q Wrens made a nest and laid eggs on my front-door wreath. What's the best way to handle the situation?
Gloria Sfameni CITRUS HILLS, FLORIDA

Kenn and Kimberly: Because native birds such as wrens are protected by law, it's illegal to destroy or move their nests. Songbirds that nest around houses may become tolerant of the presence of humans, so you may be able to open and close the door gently without disturbing them. Or use another door until the eggs hatch and the young wrens leave the nest, which should take less than a month. If neither of those options will work, contact your state wildlife agency and ask what you should do.

Pileated
woodpecker

Q Is it normal to see three pileated woodpeckers together?

Libba Fairleigh
BLACK MOUNTAIN, NORTH CAROLINA

Kenn and Kimberly: Seeing two pileated woodpeckers together is normal because mated pairs often stay together all year. But it's much more unusual to see three together. A few circumstances could explain this. In late summer or early fall, young pileated woodpeckers may still be associating with their parents. During winter, adults may be less defensive of their territory, so they may allow intruders to linger.

MEET THE EXPERTS

Kenn and Kimberly Kaufman are the duo behind the Kaufman Field Guide series. They speak and lead bird trips all over the world.

Melinda Myers is a nationally known, award-winning garden expert, TV/radio host and author of more than 20 books.

Grow for Your Zone

Find the number associated with your region,
and stick to plants that will thrive in your area

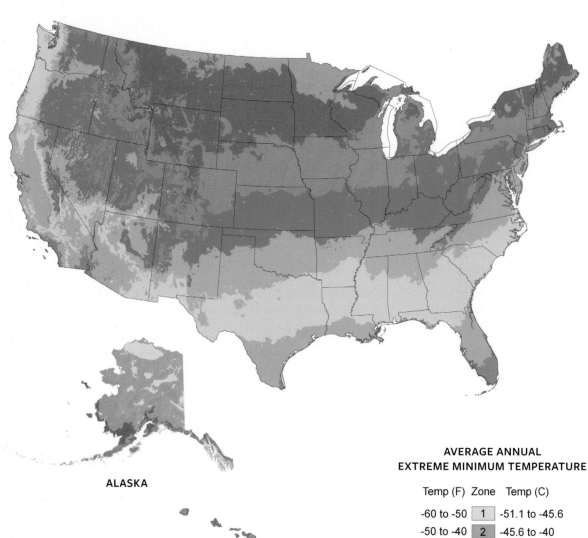

ALASKA

HAWAII

USDA PLANT HARDINESS ZONES

Hardiness zones reflect the average annual
minimum cold temperatures for an area. If it's
difficult to precisely locate your city on the map
above, use the interactive version on the USDA
website, *planthardiness.ars.usda.gov*. Enter your
ZIP code, then your hardiness zone and average
minimum winter temperature range will appear.

Birdhouse Guidelines

Discover which dwellings are best for your backyard birds

SPECIES	DIMENSIONS (LxWxH)	HOLE	PLACEMENT	COLOR	NOTES
Eastern bluebird	5″x5″x8″	1½″ centered 6″ above floor	5′-10′ high in an open sunny area	light earth tones	likes open areas, especially facing a field
Tree swallow	5″x5″x6″	1½″ centered 4″ above floor	5′-8′ high in the open; 50-100% sun	light earth tones or gray	within 2 miles of a pond or lake
Purple martin	multiple apartments 6″x6″x6″each	2⅛″ centered 2¼″ above floor	15′-20′ high in the open	white	open yard without tall trees; near water
Tufted titmouse	4″x4″x8″	1¼″ centered 6″ above floor	4′-10′ high	light earth tones	prefers to live in or near woods
Chickadee	4″x4″x8″ or 5″x5″x8″	1⅛″ centered 6″ above floor	4′-8′ high	light earth tones	small tree thicket
Nuthatch	4″x4″x10″	1¼″ centered 7½″ above floor	12′-25′ high on tree trunk	bark-covered or natural	prefers to live in or near woods
House wren	4″x4″x8″ or 4″x6″x8″	1″ centered 6″ above floor	5′-10′ high on post or hung in tree	light earth tones or white	prefers lower branches of backyard trees
Northern flicker	7″x7″x18″	2½″ centered 14″ above floor	8′-20′ high	light earth tones	put 4″ of sawdust inside for nesting
Downy woodpecker	4″x4″x10″	1¼″ centered 7½″ above floor	12′-25′ high on tree trunk	simulate natural cavity	prefers own excavation; provide sawdust
Red-headed woodpecker	6″x6″x15″	2″ centered 6″-8″ above floor	8′-20′ high on post or tree trunk	simulate natural cavity	needs sawdust for nesting
Wood duck	10″x10″x24″	4″x3″ elliptical 20″ above floor	2′-5′ high on post over water or 12′-40′ high on tree facing water	light earth tones or natural	needs 3-4″ of sawdust or shavings for nesting
American kestrel	10′x10″x24″	4x3″ elliptical 20″ above floor	12′-40′ high on post or tree trunk	light earth tones or natural	needs open approach on edge of woodlot or in isolated tree
Screech-owl	10″x10″x24″	4x3″ elliptical 20″ above floor	12′-40′ high on tree	light earth tones or natural	prefers open woods or edge of woodlot

Note: With the exception of wrens and purple martins, birds do not tolerate swaying birdhouses. Birdhouses should be firmly anchored to a post, a tree or the side of a building.

Source: *Garden Birds of America* by George H. Harrison. Willow Creek Press, 1996.

Nest Boxes to Know

Welcome more bird families to your backyard with a variety of cozy places for them to raise their young

WOODPECKER HOUSE

Entice woodpeckers with boxes attached to tree trunks, placing boxes 8 to 25 feet high. Add 4 inches of wood shavings to the floor for woodpeckers to use as nesting material. Vary the size of the entrance hole based on species: Downies like 1¼ inches; flickers favor 2½ inches.

SONGBIRD HOUSE

Chickadees, titmice, bluebirds and wrens are the most common backyard cavity nesters. They'll take up residence in classic wood birdhouses, but they're very particular about the size of the entrance hole. These songbirds are most likely to raise a family in a box if the hole is 1 to 1½ inches in diameter.

SCREECH-OWL HOUSE

Hang a box for screech-owls to nest in during summer and roost in during winter. They'll use a house with an elliptical entrance hole that's 4 inches wide by 3 inches high. Watch them peek their heads out near dusk. Bonus! Wood ducks enjoy the same type of birdhouse.

PURPLE MARTIN HOUSE

Purple martins nest in colonies, so consider a house with 6 to 12 cavities. Being a martin landlord takes some commitment, though. First set up a large multi-unit house 15 to 20 feet above ground, and then keep the cavities clear of nonnative house sparrows.

BUY OR BUILD

Find birdhouses at your local big-box store, or look for a pattern online and make your own.

Birds and Their Favorite Foods

	Nyjer (thistle) seed	Cracked corn	White proso millet	Black oil sunflower seed	Hulled sunflower seed	Beef suet	Fruit	Sugar water (nectar)*
Rose-breasted grosbeak				•	•			
Black-headed grosbeak				•	•			
Evening grosbeak		•	•	•	•			
Northern cardinal		•	•	•	•		•	
Indigo bunting	•		•		•			
Eastern towhee	•	•	•	•	•			
Dark-eyed junco	•	•	•	•	•			
White-crowned sparrow	•	•	•	•	•			
White-throated sparrow	•	•	•	•	•			
American tree sparrow	•	•	•		•			
Chipping sparrow	•	•	•		•			
Song sparrow	•	•	•		•			
House sparrow	•	•	•		•			
House finch	•	•	•	•	•			
Purple finch	•	•	•	•	•			
American goldfinch	•	•	•	•	•			
Pine siskin	•	•	•	•	•			
Scarlet tanager							•	•
Western tanager							•	•
Baltimore oriole							•	•
Red-winged blackbird		•		•	•			
Eastern bluebird							•	
Wood thrush							•	
American robin							•	
Gray catbird							•	
Northern mockingbird							•	
Brown thrasher							•	
Ruby-throated hummingbird								•
Anna's hummingbird								•
Broad-tailed hummingbird								•
Tufted titmouse	•			•	•	•		
Black-capped chickadee	•			•	•	•		
White-breasted nuthatch						•		
Carolina wren						•		
Cedar waxwing							•	
Woodpecker				•	•	•	•	
Scrub-jay		•		•	•	•	•	
Blue jay		•		•	•	•	•	
Mourning dove	•	•	•		•			
Northern bobwhite		•	•		•			
Ring-necked pheasant		•	•					
Canada goose		•						
Mallard		•						

* To make sugar water, mix 4 parts water with 1 part sugar. Boil, cool and serve.
Store leftovers in the refrigerator for up to a week. Change feeder nectar every three to five days.

Source: *Garden Birds of America* by George H. Harrison. Willow Creek Press, 1996.

Choose a Seed Feeder

Use an option that attracts the birds you want to spot in your backyard

HOPPER

This classic feeder is often in the shape of a house or barn and holds enough seed to feed birds for days. Hoppers are a surefire way to offer black oil sunflower seeds to finches, jays, cardinals, buntings and other perching birds. Many have suet cages on two sides, making them all-purpose feeders for every season.

TUBE

Tube feeders are available with small ports for thistle seed or larger ports for sunflower, safflower and mixed seeds. If you want to attract small, clinging birds such as chickadees, titmice and finches, look for a tube feeder with small perches under the ports. The perches discourage bully birds and squirrels.

THISTLE

Designed to hold tiny thistle seeds (also sold as Nyjer seeds), thistle feeders are a major draw for goldfinches. Feeders range from simple hanging mesh bags to plastic or metal tubes. You can even get ones that are a few feet long to feed an entire flock of finches or redpolls. Look for a thistle feeder that's easy to clean, as the small seeds can collect mold in enclosed tubes.

PLATFORM

These feeders hang from a tree branch or sit atop legs on the ground, and they are always completely open. This gives large birds enough space to land and eat. Sparrows, jays, juncos and blackbirds visit platform feeders, but so do squirrels.

Find feeders such as these, and more, at a big-box store, garden center, specialty bird store or online.

I live on a secluded property by a lake in the lower Adirondacks. The back edge of the yard is lined with flowering shrubs and trees, such as this cherry tree. A large variety of warblers visit the area, but yellow warblers are my favorite.

Lisa Young HADLEY, NEW YORK

Birds&Blooms